Roger Fowler

An introduction to
Transformational Syntax

Routledge & Kegan Paul London

First published in Great Britain 1971
by Routledge and Kegan Paul Ltd.
Broadway House
68–74 Carter Lane
London, EC4V 5EL
Printed in Great Britain by
The Camelot Press Ltd
London & Southampton
and set in Monotype Times New Roman,
10 point, 1 point leaded
© Roger Fowler, 1971

ISBN 0 7100 6975 8 (c)
ISBN 0 7100 6976 6 (p)

c

Contents

Preface

This is a textbook on transformational-generative syntax, a mode of grammatical description proposed by the American linguist Noam Chomsky in a little book called *Syntactic Structures* published in 1957. Since that time, TG, as it has come to be called, has undergone massive growth and change. In the first place, its general framework has become accepted by the majority of Western linguists as providing the most reliable and revealing version of linguistic analysis. This fact has to be acknowledged despite intractable opposition from a few representatives of older schools of linguistics or of more insular traditions; and despite many disagreements about details of the proposed analysis. Second, TG has benefited from very substantial and useful revisions over the years.

The net consequence of these developments is that, although there is an increasingly wide demand for information on TG, current writings in the field are forbiddingly specialized and somewhat disputatious, and the older books have become somewhat out of date. Available elementary textbooks fall into two categories: there are those which were published in the early and mid-1960s, and project a version of TG which is not entirely consonant with more recent statements of the approach; and there are newer books – an increasing number – which embody fragments of contemporary revisions in what is sometimes a puzzling way. I have attempted to provide a 'compromise' account. The primary intention is to describe a transformational model of syntax which is more up to date than the classic textbooks, based as they are on *Syntactic Structures*, can provide. In essence, this means incorporating the general changes announced in Chomsky's *Aspects of the Theory of Syntax* (1965) and foreshadowed in Katz and Postal's *Integrated Theory of Linguistic*

Descriptions (1964). At the same time, I have tried to avoid making *Syntactic Structures* 'unreadable' through uncompromising paraphrase of *Aspects*: I assume that any student who uses the present book as a way of gaining access to contemporary syntactic theory will be interested enough to read *Syntactic Structures*, which, though now superseded in many respects, remains the most succinct, powerful and attractive argument for a transformational approach to syntax.

Readers who are familiar with the history of TG will soon realize that the present book is not a faithful paraphrase of *Aspects*. I would claim that it builds on the basic framework of that account – although even that claim may be controversial. Prematurely, I feel, the whole position of *Aspects* is under attack from some quarters. What I have tried to do is tidy up such contradictions and omissions as appear in *Aspects* without, in my opinion, invalidating the overall position. In an attempt to reflect contemporary work I have gone beyond the letter of *Aspects* (hence my reading of it could be called inaccurate) in several respects: a more extensive use of feature analysis in syntax, and, in particular, a new treatment of *Det* and *Aux* which is not envisaged in *Aspects*. Beyond this up-dating of *Aspects*, I have tried to indicate directions of subsequent enquiry by other grammarians: for this reason, my treatment of pronouns, relative and appositive clauses, and conjoining has been worded in a tentative and open-ended way – these are current preoccupations in syntactic research and I want to suggest that further rethinking in these areas may bring important and radical revisions to the very basis of the grammar.

The grammar presented here, then, is by no stretch of the imagination 'final': it is a provisional grammar designed to help students read both classic and contemporary writings in TG. Certain obvious limitations of the present model of syntax make it clear that it is quite provisional: I would point especially to the difficulty of explaining adverbials and phrasal conjunction in this version of transformational syntax. A student who realizes just what these particular difficulties are will be well equipped to evaluate both older and newer solutions to such problems.

A word on how this book is to be read. It is a textbook and an instrument, to be used rather than consulted. The material is presented sequentially, with modifications *en route*, and so it should be read slowly, from beginning to end. It is not a reference book, and, to discourage its use as such, the index is minimal. I assume that the book will normally be used in a taught course, in conjunction with other reading materials. At the end of the book there is a short reading list: this reflects a range of important books and articles which any student who has mastered this book might be expected to have read by the time he finishes his course. The teacher of a course on TG which uses this book will certainly want to assign particular readings chapter by chapter, and I would not wish to dictate what these should be, so have not made many specific recommendations. Likewise, the topics for discussion and exercises at the end of each chapter are, by and large, posed rather neutrally: most of them can be attempted using analytic terms which are not precisely those offered in this book. They can be supplemented by more detailed analytic tasks slanted towards different techniques of analysis.

The book contains no footnotes, because I think it will be easier to read without continual qualifications and references. However, I would not wish to conceal the fact that the materials are not on the whole original, but drawn eclectically from a wide range of authors within the general TG framework. The responsibility for their presentation, and certainly for the overall content of the book, is mine alone.

Of the many people who have helped me determine the content and organization of this book, I would particularly like to thank several generations of students of linguistics at the University of California (Berkeley) and the University of East Anglia, who have had this material tested on them in oral form and who, directly and indirectly, have been responsible for modifications too numerous to itemize but nevertheless quite invaluable.

one

What is a Grammar?

The word 'grammar' in present-day linguistics has at least two important meanings. On the one hand, we say that a speaker knows the grammar of his language. He usually does not know it consciously – unless he has some special training in linguistics, he cannot talk confidently about the nature of his grammar. A grammar in this first sense comprises the linguistic knowledge speakers possess which enables them to communicate in their language. 'Grammar' here is a psychological, mentalistic, concept. The second sense relates to the linguist, not to the speaker: the linguist is said to write a grammar of the language. This grammar is a formal, explicit, description of the language.

Now these two usages must be kept apart. One look at a printed grammar is enough to convince us that it is extremely unlikely that the speaker knows *his* grammar as an object of the shape the linguist provides when he writes *his* grammar. If we could magically 'tap' the speaker's hidden linguistic knowledge – by hypnosis, drugs or whatever other implausible technique – so that he could tell us directly what it is that he knows which we refer to as 'his grammar', he would not simply dictate Jespersen's *Modern English Grammar* or Chomsky's *Syntactic Structures* to us. The speaker does not store his linguistic knowledge in the format which the linguist adopts for explanatory purposes; nor, when he produces sentences, does he follow step-by-step the processes which the linguist spells out as he constructs derivations for sentences. This latter point is most important, and I will return to it: a linguist's grammar *generates* sentences; a speaker *produces* (and understands) sentences – the two processes are quite independent.

Although the two senses of 'grammar' must be dissociated, we can

1

learn a lot about how to write a grammar, and what to put in it, by speculating on the nature of the grammatical knowledge of speakers. We can profitably ask: what must a speaker–hearer know in order to communicate in his language? If we observe linguistic behaviour from a number of angles, we can begin to make observations which encourage us to predict certain necessary components of grammatical knowledge. First, native speakers know that, of the following three sentences, (1) is not a sentence of English, (2) is an ungrammatical sentence of English, (3) is a grammatical sentence of English:

(1) Quel est l'objet à la fois intégral et concret de la linguistique?
(2) Three tons are weighed by this truck.
(3) This truck weighs three tons.

To go into more detail, they know more about ungrammatical sentences; for example, that (4), (5), (6) and (7) are progressively more deviant:

(4) This circle is square.
(5) John alarmed an apple.
(6) John alarmed a the.
(7) Alarmed a the John.

More relevantly, perhaps, they know an enormous amount about grammatical sentences of English. For example, they know that (8) and (9) are similar in meaning, as are (10), (11) and (12) and, in a different way, (13) and (14):

(8) Her frankness astonished him.
(9) He was astonished by her frankness.
(10) The carpet was brown.
(11) The brown carpet . . .
(12) The carpet which was brown . . .
(13) He mounted his proud horse.
(14) He mounted his proud steed.

It goes without saying, of course, that speakers know which sentences are different, as well as which ones are alike. That is, they can tell sentences apart. This observation needs no illustration at this point, since the book as a whole is a discourse upon it.

Another area of linguistic knowledge concerns ambiguous sentences. Consider the following two examples:

(15) The chicken is ready to eat.
(16) I saw her in the street.

(15) can be associated with either 'X eats the chicken' or 'the chicken

2

eats X'. (16) means either 'I saw her when I was in the street' or 'I saw her when she was in the street'. A mature speaker of English knows enough about the structure of (15) and (16) to retrieve either (or, as alternatives, both) of the meanings for each of these sentences.

The linguist attempts to find a way of explaining these facts about speaker–hearers' linguistic capacities. He has to account for the structure of English sentences in a way which takes cognizance of speakers' intuitions of deviance, similarity, distinctness and ambiguity in their experience of English sentences. For instance, no analysis of (15) is adequate unless it assigns two alternative structural descriptions to that sentence, in recognition of the fact that speakers attach two different meanings to it. In this case, the grammarian will probably say that *the chicken* is the Object of the verb in one interpretation ('X eats the chicken'), the Subject of the sentence in the other ('The chicken eats X'). 'Subject' and 'Object' are descriptive concepts which the linguist proposes as a way of explaining certain structural facts about English. Notice that, while the motivation for these concepts comes from an enquiry into 'what the speaker knows' – here, the speaker's perception of ambiguity – they are no more than theoretical terms, aids to expressing a hypothesis about linguistic knowledge. It is not necessary to assume that English speakers' brains contain two compartments labelled 'Subject' and 'Object'.

A linguist writes a grammar in an attempt to expose the structure of the sentences of a language. His structural analysis is well-motivated to the extent that he bears in mind that this set of sentences relates to a shared linguistic competence in speakers of the language under description. The problem 'What do speakers know?' has an immense bearing on our more directly relevant question 'How shall I present the structure of the sentences by which speakers communicate?'

Briefly, a language *L* is a set of sentences. The linguist must account for all and only the grammatical sentences of *L*. ('*L*' is a standard abbreviation for 'any natural language'.) This obligation follows from my comments on sentences (1)–(3) above: the mature speaker–hearer can distinguish between grammatical sentences of *L*, ungrammatical sentences of *L*, and sentences which are not of *L*. If the set described did not have limits, the grammar produced would be utterly unprincipled: it would fail to divide off English from French sentences, and, since it would omit to separate off ungrammatical and grammatical sentences of *L*, it would be structurally anarchic. I will assume that we have procedures for discounting sentences which are not of *L* and sentences which are not grammatical sentences of *L*. (Actually, these procedures are not yet properly established, but the problems are too complex to be discussed here.) If we can thus recognize grammatical sentences of *L*, we must go on to ask 'How many of them are there?' The answer to this question is known: the set *L* contains an infinite number of grammatical sentences. Almost every sentence we hear, or produce, is new to us. We are not normally conscious of the inventiveness of natural language; do not realize that few of our sentences are exact repetitions of already-used utterances. Of course, every society has a stock of routine utterances like 'Good morning', 'Dear Sir', 'Thank you', 'No Smoking', 'I love you', 'Any other business?' and so on. These utterances, which are frequently used, invariant, and tied to ritualized communication situations, are quite untypical of normal linguistic performance, which is diversified apparently without limit. One might object that this observation is either unprovable, or, if provable, irrelevant, since, because of human mortality, we cannot actually experience an infinite set of sentences. However, we need this assumption, because we must account for the creativity of language – we are interested in the newness of sentences, even if we cannot be concerned with their infiniteness. And there is, as it happens, a demonstration of the notion 'infinite set of sentences' which is not vulnerable to the embarrassing death of the grammarian before he finishes counting sentences. What we can show is that there is *no longest sentence* in a natural language, and therefore by implication that there are an infinite number of sentences. (This is not to say that there can be a sentence of infinite length, as has sometimes been claimed, quite erroneously.) For every sentence of the type (17), a longer sentence (18) is possible:

(17)   John eats meat and vegetables.
(18)   John eats meat, vegetables and fruit.

And for every sentence (18), a longer sentence can be constructed by adding one more item. I will give two more examples of constructions with this property; there are in fact several syntactic devices available for extending sentences indefinitely:

(19)   John believed that Mary claimed that Peter maintained that Clive said that . . .
(20)   This hot, sunny, lazy, predictable . . . climate suits me very well.

As the sentences of a language are infinite in number, the set which the linguist must describe cannot be coextensive with any finite corpus of sentences which, by observation and recording, he might collect. There is a second reason why the task of writing a grammar cannot be accomplished by merely cataloguing the structures found in an observed corpus of sentences. The fact is that the actual utter-

4

ances of speakers do not adequately reflect speakers' real competence in *L*. Actual speech, as any unprejudiced observation will confirm, is riddled with grammatical mistakes of all kinds: incomplete sentences, false concords, arbitrary changes of structure in mid-sentence, illicit conjoinings of constituents which ought not to be linked together – or at least not in the manner that they are – and so on. (I am not appealing to 'prescriptive' standards. By 'ungrammatical' here I don't mean structures which, in the manner of the eighteenth-century purifiers or the edicts of the French Academy, have been decreed to be unacceptable; but structures which native speakers, if they could be reliably consulted, would agree are ill-formed from the standpoint of their grammatical knowledge.) These errors stem from various kinds of psychological and situational 'interference': distraction, lapses of memory, shifts of attention, hesitation, etc. To describe such deviant sentences as these which occur in a corpus would be to describe linguistically irrelevant psychological factors as well as the linguistically relevant structural knowledge of speakers.

Thus a corpus of utterances is not the true subject-matter of linguistic description: it is only *data*—a set of observations from which, with caution, the linguist must draw his grammatical statements. In view of what has just been said, it is clear that the linguist's use of his primary data must involve two adaptations. First, some 'idealization' is necessary so that the grammar does not take account of the deviant sentences which occur in the corpus. Second, the linguist must devise rules which project from his finite, observed materials to an infinite set of sentences. That is to say, the grammar must have *predictive* power.

All this adds up to the fact that a grammar is not a simple reflection of linguistic usage. A few years ago, linguists used to be attacked, for instance in the editorials of educational journals, for abandoning all standards and saying that 'anything goes': in fact, linguists until quite recently believed that any sentence which was produced ought to be described by a grammar. But now a major reorientation has taken place – it has been realized that speakers' actual linguistic performance is not a very accurate indication of their underlying linguistic competence. Many features of linguistic performance, many aspects of texts and utterances, have to be discounted when writing a grammar. At this stage, I might mention just one other characteristic of discourse which a grammar does not seek to represent. It is well known that some words, and some constructions, occur more frequently than others: e.g. words like *the* and *and* are much more frequent than *discourse* or *dog*; complex sentences more frequent than simple sentences. Furthermore, the types of sentences which occur in discourse correlate broadly with the circumstances in which discourse is used – there are typical styles for advertising, informal conversation, political rhetoric, scientific writing, etc. But as far as the grammar is concerned, no one sentence, or type of sentence, is more predictable than any other. Grammar does not take account of probabilities. If a sentence occurs in a text or discourse, the grammar will describe its structure; it will not explain why that sentence rather than some other was selected. The explanation of *why* sentences occur in discourse is the task of stylistics and sociolinguistics, not of grammar.

A grammar which meets the requirements outlined above is called a *generative* grammar. Such a grammar is predictive or projective in the sense that, given a finite body of data (including a collection of observed sentences), it offers a system of rules so framed as to account for an infinite set of potential sentences. In this way a grammar 'generates' or 'enumerates' or 'describes' or 'defines' the set of sentences which makes up the language. In an explicit and formal manner, the grammar assigns at least one structural description to each sentence in the language (allowing that many sentences are ambiguous and must therefore receive two or more structural descriptions). We can test individual sentences – 'Is this sentence generated by the grammar of English?' – by retracing a formal derivation: by working through a series of rule-applications by which the sentence is derived. (For the notion of 'derivation', see below, pp. 45–7.) A generative grammar allows each structural description to be associated unambiguously with one derivation. Remember that a derivation is *not* an account of how a speaker produces a sentence. As we will see when we have looked at some derivations, such a proposal would be completely nonsensical. Early critics of transformational-generative grammar believed, quite mistakenly, that 'generate' meant 'produce' – that such a grammar focused on the speaker's end of the communicative process. Actually, a generative grammar is quite neutral with respect to speaker or hearer: it makes no claims to explain how a sentence in actual linguistic performance is either produced or comprehended.

One further clarification of terminology is necessary. A generative grammar does not have to be a transformational grammar. 'Transformation' refers to a particular kind of rule, and a generative grammar may or may not utilize transformational rules. In practice, most modern generative grammars happen also to be transformational. But in principle a generative grammar without transformational rules could be written. We may note also that transformations are not restricted to syntax: there are transformational rules in phonology, also. Note that the present book is about transformational *syntax*, and this is not the same as transformational *grammar* because grammar includes more than syntax.

I have said that a generative grammar 'assigns structural descriptions to sentences' and that in this way the linguist accounts for their structure in a manner which is consistent with what he can deduce about speaker–hearers' linguistic knowledge. We must now ask 'What do structural descriptions [*SDs*] tell us about sentences?' Given any one of the infinite set of sentences of *L*, all fully competent speakers of that language will agree, within reasonable limits, on its meaning. Equally, discounting peculiarities of accent and personal voice quality, speakers agree on what it sounds like. To put it another way, speakers are able to correctly associate a *semantic interpretation* with a *phonetic representation* for each of an infinite set of sentences of *L*. It would seem reasonable to expect a structural description to reveal those qualities which speakers attribute to sentences as they achieve sound-meaning associations. Let us consider a simple sentence:

(21)   The cat sat on the mat

is readily interpretable somewhat as follows: it concerns a cat (known to be a certain kind of animal), particularized as one cat (rather than as more than one) and as a specific cat rather than any old cat (*the*, not *a*); identifiable behaviour (sitting) is attributed to the cat; a location is specified; this location is identified as a particular kind of inanimate object; the position of the cat relative to this object is given ('on'); the whole semantic complex – cat-sitting-location-mat – is set in past time. All this is roughly what the sentence means, to any unprejudiced English speaker. He possesses conventions for constructing this meaning, and he is also able to give these conventions realization in sound or script. These conventions of meaning and sound are community property: for every sentence, all speakers in the community agree on the mechanisms by which meanings are built up and associated with sounds.

Generative linguists, like traditional grammarians in general, deal with these facts by setting up three interrelated levels of description: a *semantic* level, a *syntactic* level and a *phonological* level. Alternatively, we could say that a grammar has three 'components', calling the components by their traditional names. (Note that 'grammar' is often used as an equivalent to 'syntax'; but our usage of the term 'grammar' is, perhaps *un*traditionally, more inclusive.) The *semantic* component is responsible, first, for assigning meanings to lexical items: it must incorporate a dictionary. Like ordinary dictionaries, this one must attempt to distinguish each lexical item from all others, by stating exactly what senses mature speakers attribute to each item in the language's vocabulary. It must also try to set out the *structure* of the lexicon: the semantic relations (synonymy, antonymy, superordination, etc.) which exist between lexical items. A thesaurus aims to show these relationships, but conventional dictionaries do not usually attempt to define such relationships systematically. Second, the semantic component of a grammar should account for the fact that the meanings of individual words are, in sentences, amalgamated so that more complex meanings are formed. Since these 'larger' meanings are built up under syntactic constraints, the semantic component has to be arranged so that it can make reference to appropriate syntactic properties of sentences. The general design of the *syntactic* component of a grammar will be indicated in some detail in the next chapter. To put it in rather impressionistic terms, syntax distributes lexical items – and non-lexical formatives – in patterns, patterns which are spread out 'left-to-right' in time or space. Syntax lays the basis for translating an abstract meaning-complex into a piece of sequential behaviour. It does so by generating a linear string of words arranged in a regular pattern. This string constitutes the input to the *phonological* component of the grammar. For every word, and every string of words, there is an agreed realization in sound, a phonetic shape. The phonological component specifies what phonetic contour is to be attached to each of the infinite number of strings of words that the semantic and syntactic parts of the grammar produce between them. It is a set of instructions for pronunciation. Since many languages use a written, as well as spoken, medium, there is also a *graphological* equivalent to the phonological section of the grammar.

This book is about syntax. It will therefore have little to say about the details of phonological and semantic structure. But we must remember that the three components interlock, that none of them functions independently of the others. I have already mentioned, for example, that semantics must make reference to syntax to guide the formation of sentence-meanings out of the sub-sentence elements provided by the dictionary. Likewise, the phonological component cannot work unless it has a very precise analysis of the syntactic structure of the sentences for which it has to design a phonetic representation. Syntax is very definitely not autonomous, and so during the course of this book I will do my best to clarify the points at which it makes contact with the other components.

Exercises and topics for discussion

1. Discuss the distinction between 'prescriptive' and 'descriptive' grammar.

2. In Ch. 1, some of the reasons why a grammar cannot be simply a description of a finite corpus were given. Work out the arguments against 'corpus-bound' grammar in more detail.

3. Investigate the notion of 'grammaticalness' in the writings of some modern transformational grammarians.

4. Make a critical review of Noam Chomsky's expositions of the distinction between 'linguistic competence' and 'linguistic performance'. You may wish to consider also Ferdinand de Saussure's distinction between *langue* and *parole*.

two

Deep and Surface Structure

As it happens, the most important relationship between syntax, semantics and phonology can be presented straight away. The linguistic levels of 'meaning' and 'sound' both have to be invoked to help us define the central distinction in syntax – and with it the idea of a transformational grammar itself. Consider the following sentences:

(22)   He took off his hat.
(23)   He took his hat off.

These sentences have the same meaning; but they are different arrangements of words. Since the difference between (22) and (23) is immediately apparent at first glance, 'on the surface', as it were, let us say that (22) and (23) exhibit different *surface structures* (or *superficial structures*). To continue the metaphor, we will explain the synonymy of (22) and (23) by saying that they have the same *deep structure* (or *underlying structure*). Deep structure relates to meaning; surface structure relates to order of elements, and hence to sound, for in effect the surface structure determines the sequence of sounds which occurs in a phonetic realization of a sentence. Surface structure is a dimension with physical associations, since it is the point at which a sentence impinges on space and time. Deep structure, however, is an abstraction, a complex of meanings which is 'unpronounceable' unless it is rendered as a surface structure. Before we attempt to say more about the theoretical status of deep and surface structures, let us look at some more examples.

(22) and (23) illustrate the situation in which one deep structure is realized as two different surface structures. Another type of example of this same relationship is (24), (25) and (26):

(24)   The black cat sat on the mat.
(25)   The cat, which was black, sat on the mat.
(26)   The cat sat on the mat. The cat was black.

All three of the sentences – in the case of (26), pair of sentences – express the same structure of meanings. In (24)–(26) a cat is said to have been black and the same cat is said to have sat on a mat. Although (25) is longer than (24), it adds no meaning; although (26) splits the statement into two distinct sentences, it does not alter the meaning-relationships within the statement – it would be an extremely perverse interpretation to claim that two different cats are mentioned in (26). So, as in (22) and (23), a set of utterances with quite dissimilar surface structures is found to contain the same deep structure.

The reverse situation may be found too: one surface structure may hide the presence of two or more deep structures. I refer to the class of syntactically ambiguous sentences, already represented above:

(15)   The chicken is ready to eat.
(16)   I saw her in the street.

We cannot pronounce (15) one way to show that *the chicken* is the Object of *eat*, another way to emphasize that it is the Subject. In (16), *in the street* goes with *I* in one interpretation, *her* in another – the two interpretations sound just the same: one surface structure, but undeniably two meanings. A favourite example of transformationalists is the following pair:

(27)   John is easy to please.
(28)   John is eager to please.

These two sentences appear to be identical except for the simple lexical contrast *easy/eager*. But there is a fundamental difference: in (27) *John* stands in an Object–verb relation to *please*; in (28) *John* is in a Subject–verb relation to *please*. Compare *It is easy to please John* with (27); but *It is eager to please John* is not in a meaningful relation to (28). (Notice that the two different functions of *ready* in the sentence about the chicken are represented separately in *easy* and *eager*, neither of which is the syntactic chameleon that *ready* is.)

Obviously, a grammarian who paid attention only to surface structure would fail to notice some vitally important distinctions – between (27) and (28), between the two meanings of (15) and between the two meanings of (16). The familiar operation of 'parsing' would miss the point entirely. Parsing entails assigning each word in a sentence to a part of speech or word-class, and then representing the sentence as a sequence of these word-classes. On this analysis, (15), (27) and (28) would all come out as

Noun + Copula + Adjective + Particle + Verb

Or, bracketing together items which go together to form one unit,

(Noun + (Copula + (Adjective + (Particle + Verb))))

Alternatively, we might use notions like 'Subject' and 'Object'; but that way *John* in (27) and *the chicken* on one reading of (15) would be erroneously labelled, since we would certainly be tempted to call *John* and *the chicken* 'Subject' in all cases. Similarly, *He* in (9) would be wrongly called 'Subject':

(9)   He was astonished by her frankness.

But in (9), despite appearances, *her frankness* is the 'real' Subject, as it is in (8), in which it is also the superficial Subject:

(8)   Her frankness astonished him.

To return to our original example (22) versus (23), an analysis by parsing would again misrepresent the syntactic facts. (22) would be

Pronoun + Verb + Particle + Possessive Pronoun + Noun

and (23):

Pronoun + Verb + Possessive Pronoun + Noun + Particle

Two analyses, but one meaning. Parsing shows how (22) and (23) differ, but not how they are the same. What is wrong with the analysis of (23), of course, is that it obscures the fact that *took* and *off* form, semantically, one unitary constituent (cf. *remove*) like *put away* (*store*), *run up* (*accumulate*), *put down* (*suppress*) and many other similar English verbs. In the case of (23), we clearly need two different levels of representation. On one level, we must show that certain words occur in a certain order—if we do not show this, we cannot tell how (23) is to be spoken or written. On another level, we must show certain meanings, and meaning-relations, which are present in the sentence – this involves associating *took* and *off* semantically, whereas on the other level they must be dissociated positionally. The positional level of representation is a representation of (23) at the level of surface structure; the semantic level (which can ignore positional facts if necessary) is a representation at the level of deep structure. To complete our analysis, we must make sure that the two levels of representation are related in some rational way, and that the analysis of (23) is referable to whatever analysis is proposed for (22): specifically, that the deep structure analysis of (23) is *the same as* the deep structure analysis of (22), for, as we have seen, they have the same meaning.

Before describing the technique which fulfils these analytic requirements, I will comment briefly on the problems which it has to solve for the other sentences discussed in this chapter. For (24)–(26), we must show that all the sentences express the same meaning, and we must show how the surface structure differences among the members of this trio arise: how from one underlying representation are derived different word-orders, different words, and different lengths and apparent complexities of sentences. And we must demonstrate how all these changes occur without variation in the meaning of the statement. With (15), (16) and (27), (28) we have a mirror-image of the same problems. We must show how the same (or similar) surface structure is derived from different deep structures: how do these words, in these orders, stem from the given meanings? In addition, we need some formal way of representing the underlying meanings – as of course we do for (22)–(26); here, however, we need to refer explicitly to the meanings of the sentences in order to express the contrasts involved. Obviously, deep structure is determined in part by the meanings of the lexical items which occur, so we need a method of stating formally dictionary meanings. But as our examination of the sentences concerned has shown, certain syntactic functions and relations also contribute to the establishment of meaning in deep structure. The notions 'Subject' and 'Object', it appears, are critical to distinguishing (27) and (28), and the two meanings of (15). Evidently, any adequate theory of the nature of deep structure must be prepared to give sense to these concepts and to identify them in actual sentences. Moreover, it must distinguish deep structure functions (e.g. Subject) from surface structure constituents which appear to have these same functions: for example, it must allow one to decide that *John* is not the underlying Subject of (27), nor *He* that of (9). (The conventional distinction between 'logical subject' and 'grammatical subject' is relevant to these cases: for 'logical subject' read 'Subject in deep structure'; for 'grammatical', 'Subject in surface structure'.) To give this criterion a more general and more popular formulation, we might say that a theory of deep structure should allow us to decide what aspects of overt syntactic ordering are significant and what are insignificant or misleading. In (23) the separation of *took* and *off* is a red herring, as far as meaning is concerned. (22), in which *took* and *off* are adjacent, reflects the unity of the verb much more directly. As a final example, a sufficient theory of deep structure will tell us that *black* and *cat* in (24)–(26) are in a semantically relevant relationship, despite the fact that in surface structure they relate to each other in three different ways, and that

13

this diversity of physical arrangement is immaterial to the meaning. By the same token, a sufficient theory of surface structure should allow us to derive these various arrangements from the underlying structure in an ordered fashion. After all, surface structure may be opaque, but it is not haphazard: if it did not have principles of its own, we would hardly be able to recover deep structure from it; sentences would be uninterpretable.

Let us now look at a fresh example. In Latin, permutation of lexical items in surface structure does not affect deep structure. All of the following sentences mean 'Claudius loves the queen':

(29) Claudius reginam amat.
(30) Claudius amat reginam.
(31) Reginam Claudius amat.
(32) Reginam amat Claudius.
(33) Amat reginam Claudius.
(34) Amat Claudius reginam.

The agreement of meaning among these sentences is, of course, marked by the suffixes attached to each of the words, which establish *Claudius* as Subject and *reginam* as Object, regardless of the positions which the words occupy in surface structure. Since the verb *amat* is in the active rather than passive voice, the superficial Subject is known to be identical to the Subject in deep structure. To account for all the structural characteristics of these sentences, we clearly need two kinds of rules:

> (i) a set of rules which explains the syntactic relations and semantic relations and content common to all the sentences;
> (ii) a set of rules which explains the diversity of superficial word-orders distinguishing the sentences.

Rules of type (i) are called by various authors *phrase-structure rules, constituent-structure rules, rewriting rules* or *branching rules*. Type (ii) rules are (one form of) *transformational rules*. Sentences (29)–(34) dramatically illustrate the fact that one important property of transformational rules ('T-rules') is that they can rearrange constituents without altering meaning.

Example (23) differs from (22) in that it has undergone a repositioning transformation which has not affected (22). We may represent the process very informally, introducing the double arrow '⇒' which conventionally indicates that a T-rule is applied:

> He took off his hat ⇒ He took his hat off
> (*deep structure*)   (*surface structure*)

This presentation symbolizes a fact that has been implicit in the whole of my discussion so far: that T-rules are applied 'between' (in some sense, not necessarily a temporal sense) deep and surface structure. We must, however, disperse this metaphor 'between' by discovering (a) how to represent deep structures as abstract objects; (b) how to state T-rules as formal instructions; (c) how to represent surface structures.

Both deep and surface structures can be represented as what we call phrase-markers. Transformational rules apply to *underlying phrase-markers* to give *derived* or *superficial phrase-markers*. (Where more than one T-rule is applied, there may be *intermediate* phrase-markers also.) In the informal notation of the previous paragraph, these phrase-markers were shown as fully-fledged sentences, but this was a mere convenience. Transformations do *not* derive sentences from sentences, but P-markers from P-markers. Here is a more appropriate notation (simplified for this preliminary discussion) for the underlying phrase-marker of (23); the mode of representation is called a *tree-diagram* or *branching diagram*:

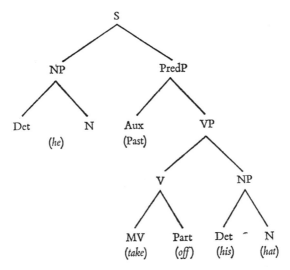

(This diagram shows the underlying phrase-marker for (22) as well as (23), since the two sentences have the same meaning. I will return to this point.) We can see in the diagram the structure of an *underlying string* obtained by listing left-to-right the items from the lowest point of each branch:

(a) *he* – Past – *take* – *off* – *his* – *hat*

The T-rule accepts (a) as input and shifts the fourth item to the rightmost position, giving a *derived string* (b):

(b) *he* – Past – *take* – *his* – *hat* – *off*

So a T-rule is an instruction which says: 'Take a string of the form (a) and perform such-and-such an operation on it, deriving a string of the form (b).' String (a) may be either underlying or intermediate; the only condition is that it must be associated with an explicit phrase-marker, for in order to produce the derived string (b) the transformational rule must be able to refer to the structure of (a).

We know that the T-rule which derives P-marker (b) from P-marker (a) – *not*, it must be stressed, 'sentence (23) from sentence (22)' – accounts for many other sentences besides (23). Compare:

(35)   The librarian put the book away.
(36)   The truck knocked the old man down.
(37)   I saw her off.
(38)   I take the clock apart.
(39)   Let's move the table over.

For economy's sake, we do not wish to reformulate a T-rule for every particular underlying string to which it applies, so the input (a) can be stated in such a way as to cover any number of pertinent cases. We can achieve this economy by referring to branching-points higher up in the tree which models the underlying phrase-marker. Thus (a_1) will serve as input to the T-rule which is behind (23), (35), (36) and (37):

(a_1) NP – Past – MV – Part – NP

(38) shows that the T-rule applies whether the sentence is in the past tense or not, so a more general representation still is possible:

(a_2) NP – Aux – MV – Part – NP

Finally, it appears from (39) that from the point of view of this transformation it is immaterial what precedes the main verb (MV); so a very general rule can be given which embraces all the cases so far examined:

X – MV – Part – NP $\Rightarrow$ X – MV – NP – Part

(X $\equiv$ 'any or no formative(s)')

This is a rule of English called the *particle-shift transformation*.

This rule does not appear in the derivation of (22) *He took off his hat*. The tree-diagram on p. 15 portrayed the underlying phrase-marker for (22) as well as (23), since the sentences have the same meaning – a common deep structure. Note that *take* and *off* are adjacent in the diagram as well as in the surface structure of (22).

Perhaps the deep and surface structures of (22) are identical. Actually, this is not the case. As we will see, there is no sentence in whose derivation there are no T-rules. The transformations which bridge underlying and superficial structures in (22) are rather too complex to show at this early stage, but a simpler sentence will illustrate the point:

(40)   I cleaned it.

At one level of generality, the underlying string is

NP – Aux – V – NP

Aux is Past, ultimately the affix (*Af*) *-ed*. In surface structure, *-ed* follows *clean*. So we propose a general affix-shifting rule

NP – Af – V – NP ⇒ NP – V – Af – NP

(alternatively, X – Af – V – Y ⇒ X – V – Af – Y, where X and Y stand for anything occurring in those positions, as did X in the particle-shift rule). This rule by definition applies also in the case of (22), although, typically, its application is not obvious in surface structure.

The claim that 'deep structure determines meaning' assumes that *all* sentences display a distinction between underlying and superficial syntax. It would be misleading and erroneous to interpret the relation between (22) and (23) as demonstrating that (23) has both deep and surface structure whereas (22), because it does not display the transformation placing *his hat* within *took off*, has only one layer of structure; or, by a similar argument, that *Her frankness astonished him* has no distinction between deep and surface structure because it has undergone no transformation of the kind which forces us to draw a line between deep and surface structure in the case of *He was astonished by her frankness*. It would be wrong to suggest that a language consists of a set of one-layered sentences such as *He took off his hat, Her frankness astonished him*, plus a set of two-layered sentences derived from them by transformation.

Distinguishing deep and surface structure is not a matter of mere analytic convenience – ease of handling sentences like *He took his hat off*, for example, through the medium of transformation. The crucial motivation, which demands that the distinction apply to *all* sentences, is that it provides a natural explanation for the fact that sound and meaning are not directly related; that the phonetic surface of linguistic symbols incorporates no intrinsic semantic properties. The separation of underlying and superficial syntax recognizes this fact by proposing that surface structure embodies all information relevant to the phonetic representation of sentences, and deep structure contains all information necessary to the semantic interpretation

17

of sentences. Thus the syntactic (transformational) route between deep and surface structure can be considered the means whereby the 'pairing' of sounds and meanings is achieved.

Transformations are responsible for the arrangement of words (or, better, *morphemes*, which are syntactic units smaller than the word) in surface structure. My discussion of (23) and of the Latin examples (29)–(34) may have suggested that the job transformations do consists of repositioning or permuting elements. In fact, transformational rules perform many different kinds of operation besides permutation. They can delete elements: for instance, it is a transformation which dispenses with the 'understood' *you* (in deep structure) of imperatives. They can insert elements, for example conjunctions and relative pronouns. They are responsible for combining units in various ways – for example, the whole apparatus of 'subordination' familiar in traditional grammar is transformationally managed: subordinate and main clauses are whole underlying P-markers linked in different ways by transformational rules. Something of the range of types of T-rule can be seen in examples (24)–(26):

(24) The black cat sat on the mat.
(25) The cat, which was black, sat on the mat.
(26) The cat sat on the mat. The cat was black.

Each of these statements seems to be based on two propositions: 'cat – sitting (on the mat)' and 'cat – black'. In this analysis, (26) appears to be the most direct expression of the underlying structure: it represents in two separate derived strings the meaning-complexes which are distinct in deep structure. We may therefore take (26) to be more 'basic' than (24) or (25): for the sake of exposition – but subject to the caution voiced above that sentences are not derived from sentences – transformations may be regarded as operating on a pair of strings something like (26) to derive (24) and (25). In (26) the Noun Phrase *the cat* is repeated for each of the two statements about the cat; in (24) and (25), where the two separate propositions are united, one occurrence of *the cat* is deleted: it is one duty of transformational rules to reduce redundancy in complex sentences by removing needless repetitions of the same item. This deletion happens as the second process in a sequential derivation which has roughly the following milestones:

(1) The cat sat on the mat. The cat was black.
(2) The cat – the cat was black – sat on the mat.
     (T-rule places the second string in the appropriate position within the first.)

18

(3) The cat – was black – sat on the mat.
   (One redundant occurrence of *NP the cat* deleted.)
(4) The cat – which was black – sat on the mat.
   (Relative pronoun inserted in the right place.)
(5) The cat, which was black, sat on the mat.
   ('Commas' inserted: actually, this T-rule provides an instruction for pronouncing the sentence with maintained or rising intonation on *cat* and *black*, thus distinguishing (25) from this, which is a different construction: (41) *The cat which was black sat on the mat*, implying that some cat which was not black did not sit on the mat. (25) is said to contain a *non-restrictive* relative clause, (41) a *restrictive* relative clause.)

The derivation for (24) demands further reduction and rearrangement. We may assume that (24), like (25), goes through stage (2) above – an assumption which has the added advantage of formally connecting pre-posed adjectives and their corresponding relative clauses. Next, everything except *black* in the 'embedded' string is deleted:

   (3a) The cat – black – sat on the mat.

Finally, the adjective is shifted to the position in front of the noun which it modifies:

   (4a) The black cat sat on the mat.

(In French, where the majority of adjectives follow nouns, this last transformational stage is unnecessary; so in French the transformational relationship between relative clauses and corresponding adjectives is much more obvious in superficial syntax.)

In this chapter we have already seen quite a range of formally distinct types of transformational rule. In later chapters, the range will be increased even more. Because of this variety in the kinds of operations performed by T-rules, it would not be very illuminating to define a transformational grammar by simply listing types of transformation. Instead, we may employ this more general definition: *a transformational grammar is a grammar which explicitly formalizes the distinction between deep and surface structure in syntax*. The transformational section of the syntax receives deep structures as its input and allows us to derive surface structures as output.

Exercises and topics for discussion

1. Collect some further examples of (a) pairs of sentences which differ in surface structure but have the same underlying structure;

19

(b) sentences which have two or more deep structures underlying one surface structure. Try to illustrate as wide a range of syntactic types as you can.

2. Read the arguments in Chomsky's *Syntactic Structures* in favour of a transformational level of analysis in syntax. He makes no reference to the concepts of deep and surface structure; how does this early exposition of his relate to the distinction in question?

3. It is a fundamental tenet of linguistics that sound and meaning are not directly related. Explore as many branches of this argument as you can.

4. A grammar should generate all of the sentences of L which are grammatical, and none of the ungrammatical ones. Reconsider the particle-shift T-rule in the light of the following sentences and of other relevant ones which may occur to you:

    (a) He took off his hat.
    (b) He took his hat off.
    (c) The truck knocked the old man down.
    (d) The truck knocked down the old man.
    (e) I saw her off.
    (f) *I saw off her.
    (g) Can you put me up?
    (h) *Can you put up me? (*Me* is not strongly stressed.)

5. Examples (29)–(34) show that Latin enjoys very free privileges for surface structure word-order; it is also a very richly inflected language. Conversely, word-order in English, a language which now has few inflexions, is quite rigidly fixed. Work out a general explanation for these facts.

An asterisk * marks deviant forms here and throughout this book.

three

Constituent Structure: Syntactic Functions

I have not yet explained what I mean by a phrase-marker. It is, of course, a kind of syntactic organization, one which can be pictured in a tree-diagram. One example of a tree-diagram was given on p. 15 above. This diagram shows two features of organization as yet un-explained: the tree 'branches' over and over again from top to bottom; and at each of the points (called *nodes*) at which the branches divide, and at each of the terminal points of the tree, there is an abbreviated label – *S, NP, N*, etc. In this and the following chapter I will show what is meant by the branching convention and by the labelling convention. When we have agreed on the motivation for, and method of, drawing tree-diagrams, we can begin to use them as a way of representing phrase-markers. Specifically, they will serve to display the structure of underlying phrase-markers.

The first point to grasp is that, although a sentence is a sequence of formatives, these formatives are not joined to another one-by-one in sequence like the links of a chain: B related to A, C related to B but not to A, D to C but not to B or A, and so on. In physical reality – spoken or written linguistic performance – words and morphemes follow one another one at a time in sequence, but this is not a reliable guide to their syntactic relationships. Syntactically, a sentence is not a simple linear concatenation of formatives like this:

(42)   The + student + s + like + the + new + library.

The sentence is rather an ordered construct in which small units are progressively built up into large on regular structural principles. It is apparent that, in sentence (42), some sub-sequences of items can be extracted which form syntactic wholes, while others would be meaningless, arbitrary, segmentations. *The students* and *like the new library* are well-formed constituents of the sentence, but *students like* and *like the* would not be. Nor would *s like*; *s* is obviously intimately connected with *student* but not at all directly related to *like*. We can show which elements 'go together' by bracketing them together:

((The (student s)) (like (the (new library))))

Each pair of brackets except the outer-most pair defines a *constituent*: a sequence of formatives which is a regular part of the structure of the next largest constituent. Thus, *new* and *library* are constituents of *new library*; *new library* and *the* are constituents of *the new library*; *like* and *the new library* are constituents of *like the new library*. *Student* and *s* are constituents of *students*, which in turn, with *the*, makes up *the students*. Finally, *the students* and *like the new library* are the constituents of the whole sentence, which itself is not, of course, a constituent of anything. Notice that some sequences (e.g. *like the*) are not bracketed together and so are not constituents; also, that any constituent is only a constituent of the 'larger' unit which *immediately* includes it. So, for instance, *new library* is not an immediate constituent of *like the new library*, although it is related to it indirectly.

We have just analysed, crudely, the constituent structure of sentence (42). If the presentation is thought to be difficult to read, we can give the same information in an unlabelled tree-diagram:

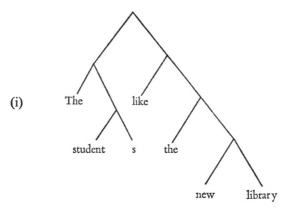

(i)

Each intersection (node) gathers together two simple or complex constituents to form one more complex unit.

Now compare the above tree-diagram with the following, which reproduces the linear analysis with plus-signs which was offered when (42) was first introduced:

(ii)

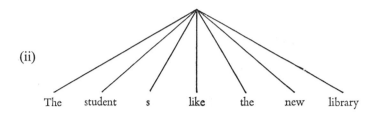

The student s like the new library

The advantage of (i) over (ii) is that it correctly acknowledges that syntactic structure is *hierarchical*, not (as shown in (ii)) linear. The concept of hierarchical structure has already been sufficiently illustrated: by it is meant that each part of a sentence joins forces with some unit of equal rank to make up a higher-order unit which dominates both of them.

Constituent structure analysis which reveals hierarchical structure brings immediate benefit to the differentiation of sentences. Linear analysis makes it impossible to tell many types of sentence apart, beyond the fact that different lexical items occur, in different orders, and in sentences of different lengths. A constituent structure analysis expressed in a branching diagram conveys at a glance structural differences among sentences; compare the shapes of the following trees:

(43)

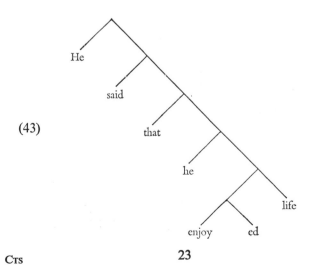

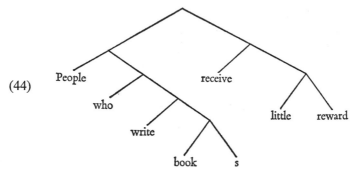

(44)

However, it has been repeatedly demonstrated that constituent analysis is not wholly adequate to the task of describing a natural language. In the above diagrams, (43) and (44) are distinguished as *superficial structures*: that is, the diagrams (similarly, the one for (42)) obscure the fact that some parts of the structure are derived transformationally, some not. Admittedly, it is a great convenience, and unobjectionable, to draw tree-diagrams of surface structures, since they offer instant, systematic, displays of the overt structural differences between sentences, and so are useful for comparative purposes. But grammars represent linguistic facts in the form of *rules*, not diagrams; and when we come to enquire what rule-applications these diagrams of derived phrase-markers imply, we find, quite naturally, that they imply a mixed bag of rules.

A constituent structure diagram must not be read as if it were based entirely on *phrase-structure rules*. Such rules, the nature of which we shall explore directly, are used to generate underlying phrase-markers. Derived phrase-markers must be seen as a result of the application of T-rules after the underlying structure has been built up by using these phrase-structure rules. The technique of tree-diagramming can become misleading unless we realize that it does not distinguish between the kinds of rules used to generate the hierarchical structures which it represents. Thus it is vital to distinguish between the rules which introduce underlying hierarchical structure and those which produce superficial constituent structure.

A phrase structure rule is always of the form

$$A \rightarrow X + Y$$

This rule-type imputes a very literal meaning to the notion of constituent structure: '*A* consists of *X* followed by *Y*'. Thus, a unit *A*, say an *NP*, has as its constituents *X* and *Y* ('Article' and 'Noun') in the order *XY*. Such a rule is reflected in a simple branching:

24

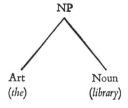

The rule for this bit of constituent structure (to be revised shortly) is

$$NP \rightarrow Art + N$$

which is a general rule of English: according to this rule, every sub-sentence structure which is an *NP* has as its constituents an Article followed by a Noun. And, of course, the configuration *Art + N* is an elementary component in deep structure meaning. But how are we to account for *the new library*? It also seems to be an *NP*, since it is freely substitutable for the simpler construction: *the students like the library/the new library*. So we might analyse *the new library* in this way:

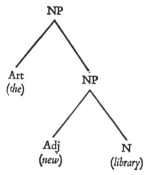

However, this analysis complicates the system of phrase structure rules, which now has to include three specifications for *NP*:

$$NP \rightarrow \begin{Bmatrix} Art + N \\ Art + NP \\ Adj + N \end{Bmatrix}$$

(The braces enclose alternative constructions.) Now we have very severely weakened the analytic concept '*NP*', particularly by blurring the distinction between adjectives and articles. Note that adjectives and articles must be assigned different distributional privileges, since we can have

25

(45)   The library was new.

but not

(46)   *The library was the.

In fact, example (45) shows us the way to identifying what is wrong with the above analysis of the phrase from (42). Although *new* is an immediate constituent of *new library* and hence an indirect constituent of *the new library*, it is a constituent which has a *transformational* relation to *library*, and is thus different in type from the constituents *the* and *library* (of *the library*) which are proper components of deep structure related by PS-rules. Compare *black* in *the black cat* discussed in the preceding chapter. Adjectives in prenominal position – (24), (42) – are surface-structure arrangements derived from adjectives in predicate position in deep structure – (26), (45).

We can put it another way. Our observations suggest that an adjective occurring before a noun has the same relationship to the noun as an adjective linked to a noun by the 'verb *to be*' has to that noun. (Compare (24) and the second sentence in (26).) To describe these two arrangements by means of two separate rules would be to obscure the fact that one relationship underlies these two word-orders. In a transformational grammar we would wish to treat one of these arrangements as basic, the other as derived. As we have just seen, the inefficiency of the rule for *NP* which includes *Adj + N* suggests that this is not the basic form. In fact, the truth of the situation seems to be that all adjectives, wherever they occur in surface structure, appear 'first' (i.e. in deep structure) in a P-marker of the form

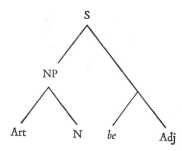

It follows that the relationship between *N* and *Adj* diagrammed by the above tree is (or is an instance of) one of the basic stock of syntactic relationships defined by that part of the grammar which generates underlying structures. Furthermore, it must be one of the syntactic relationships implicitly noted on p. 8 above when I mentioned that the semantic component of a grammar makes reference to 'appropriate syntactic properties of sentences' in building up the meaning-complexes of deep structure.

Let us now collect together the general observations that have been made so far and see what they imply for the design of the syntactic component of a grammar. The deep structure of a sentence is a set of simple P-markers containing either just one member (e.g. (8), (9), (21), (22), (23), (29)–(34), (45)) or more than one member (e.g. (16), (24), (25), (42), (43), (44)). Each of these underlying P-markers is generated by phrase-structure rules; every one is of a certain determinate constituent structure (there is no ambiguity in deep structure) and exemplifies certain fundamental syntactic properties and relations. Each of them is drawn from a small finite set of underlying P-markers generated by what we shall call the *base* of the syntactic component of the grammar, the base consisting largely of a simple phrase-structure grammar (PSG) which defines syntactic relationships and word-classes. Underlying strings are provided with lexical items collocated according to principles laid down by the semantic component. Such lexically endowed underlying P-markers are mapped on to surface structures by the transformational apparatus of the syntactic component. Transformations thus operate on semantically interpreted underlying P-markers to produce derived or superficial P-markers. These latter are surface strings of formatives which, like the underlying string(s), have constituent structure. But there are two defining differences from the structure of underlying strings: superficial strings may have apparently indeterminate structure, that is to say they may be ambiguous; and their constituent structure is accounted for by their transformational history as well as by PS-rules. Surface ambiguity implies the existence of two or more alternative transformational routes which lead 'backward' from one and the same surface structure to different deep structures.

To return now to the syntactic relationships which determine the structure of underlying P-markers. It will have been noticed that the immediate constituent analyses presented thus far have usually been based on a binary segmentation:

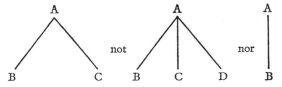

This division of one constituent into two – neither more nor less – constituents has applied whether the object of analysis has been an underlying or a superficial string. The decision to employ a principle of bipartite segmentation is neither accidental nor arbitrary. The first cut in the analysis of sentences is binary because every sentence is fundamentally a relation of two elements, a *Subject* and a *Predicate*. The analysis (47)(a) recognizes this fact; (47)(b) disguises it:

(47) (a) The children / ate the apples noisily.
      (b) The children / ate / the apples noisily.

Tentatively, we can characterize the function of predication in this way. Every sentence focuses attention, interest, enquiry, or whatever, on some 'topic' (object, event, process, concept, etc.), which is expressed as the Subject; the remainder of the sentence provides a 'comment' on this topic. In sentence (47) the Subject is 'the children'; what is predicated of the topic expressed in this Subject is that the children 'ate the apples noisily'. In so far as *ate the apples noisily* relates to *the children*, it must be considered as a unitary segment constituting as a whole the Predicate of the sentence. In the underlying 'message' of (47), the whole complex of eating, eating apples, eating apples noisily, forms one block of meaning which the syntax, through the function of predication, attributes to the children.

In (47) the Predicate is quite complex: it consists of a verb followed by an *NP* followed by an adverb. This particular complexity is not essential to predication; simpler orderings of meaning may have this function. To begin with, the adverb (*noisily*, in this case) is entirely optional – as grammarians have long noticed. We can just as easily express predication without an adverb:

(48) The children ate the apples.

(Transformationalists are uncertain about the status of adverbs, beyond knowing that, unlike the other kinds of element considered in this chapter, they are optional. Perhaps adverbs do not appear in deep structure, but are introduced by a range of transformations – a possibility to which I will return in the next chapter.) Simpler structures still – lacking the second *NP* – will also express the function of predication:

(49) The children slept.

If we compare (49) with (47), (48) we notice a difference between two types of Predicate, that containing an *Object* and that not containing an Object. Both Subject and Object are *NP*s; but they are readily distinguished in diagrams of phrase-markers in terms of the positions they occupy in trees. The distinction is obvious from the following diagram even if I do not explain the meanings of all the labels on nodes:

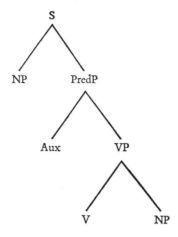

The Subject is the *NP* on the left, below a branch dominated by the node *S*; the Object is on the right, immediately dominated by the node *VP*. Notice that, if trees are properly drawn, such syntactic functions can be deduced from the shape of the tree: it is not necessary to include the terms 'Subject' and 'Object' themselves in the tree. However, one secondary test is required for 'Object', since predication may also be expressed in sentences like the following –

(50) This truck weighs three tons.
(51) John became a politician.

– in which the right-most *NP*s are not Objects. The secondary test entails submitting sentences to the passive transformation:

(52) The apples were eaten by the children.
(53) *Three tons are weighed by this truck.
(54) *A politician was become by John.

So the Object of a verb (within the Predicate) is an *NP* which is immediately dominated by *VP* and which, if the passive transformation can be applied, becomes the superficial (or 'grammatical') Subject of the derived sentence. *NP*s which do not fulfil both of these conditions are not Objects.

Two more types of Predicate are encountered, illustrated by the following:

(55) John was a politician.
(56) John was clever.

To make these Predicates consistent with those in sentences (47)–(51), we might say that they are Predicates by virtue of containing the

29

'verb *to be*'. But this interpretation does not obviously reflect the true situation. It would be quite reasonable to claim that predication in (55) and (56) is expressed by the *NP a politician* and the adjective *clever*, respectively. *Was* adds nothing to the meaning: it is semantically empty. Its function is to carry tense-information which, of course, cannot be affixed directly to *a politician* or *clever*, since they are not verbs. The underlying structure of (55) and (56) is roughly as follows:

> NP – Past – NP
> NP – Past – Adj

Because Past is, in these circumstances, 'unaffixable', an obligatory transformation is applied inserting *be* for Past to be attached to. Other transformations like this one are found elsewhere in the grammar: in particular, we may note the rule introducing *do* in negatives and questions, constructions which separate Past from the verb and so create a need for a surface structure morpheme to attach it to:

(57) Did you like the soup?
      Past – NP – V – NP
(58) You did n't like the soup.
      NP – Past – Neg – V – NP

In summary, the Predicate of a sentence need not contain a verbal element: its exponents may be a verb (49); a verb phrase containing an Object (47, 48); a verb phrase containing an *NP* which is not an Object (50, 51); an *NP* by itself (55); an adjective. These alternatives may be captured in the following rules, in which the single arrow '→' may for the moment be regarded as meaning 'consists of':

(i) S → NP + PredP
(ii) PredP → Aux + $\begin{Bmatrix} V \\ VP \\ Adj \\ NP \end{Bmatrix}$

(iii) NP → Det + N
(iv) VP → V + $\begin{Bmatrix} NP \\ Adj \end{Bmatrix}$

Rule (i) states that every underlying phrase-marker consists of a Noun Phrase followed by a Predicate Phrase. The Noun Phrase is the Subject, a fact which does not need to be stated explicitly in the rules because (a) the Subject must be an *NP*; and (b) the *NP* immediately dominated by *S* must be the Subject. (So no *NP* introduced by (ii) or (iv) could be the Subject.)

(ii) divides *PredP* into an auxiliary and one of four other constituents. For the moment, we may regard *Aux* as comprising Tense ([+Past] or [–Past]) or Tense plus a 'modal auxiliary' such as *can, will*, etc. *Aux* is separated out in this way because it applies to the whole of the *PredP*, not just to the verb (if any): for instance, in (47) the whole Predicate *ate the apples noisily* is characterized as past tense, even though it is only the verb itself which is actually marked [+Past] morphologically.

Reading from top to bottom, the bracketed choices in rule (ii) allow for (49), (48), (56) and (55).

Rule (iii) breaks down *NP* into a Determiner plus a Noun. Read in conjunction with the bottom line of rule (ii), this gives us (55) *John was a politician*, in which there are two instances of *NP*. Note that *every NP* – even a single-word *NP* such as *John* – has a Determiner; but some *Det*s are not expressed in surface structure (see Ch. 6).

(iv) expands *VP*, giving two more types of Predicate: *V + NP* as in (48) and *V + Adj* as in

(59)   John became rich.

Our simple PSG generates just five underlying phrase-markers, as follows:

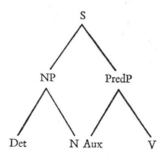

(E.g. *The children slept* by rules (i), (ii) first line, and (iii).)

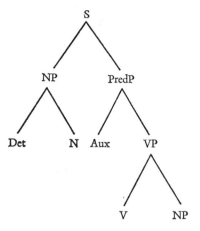

(E.g. *The children ate the apples* by rules (i), (ii) second line, (iii) twice, (iv) first line; or, by the same rules, *This truck weighs three tons* where the *VP*-dominated *NP* is not the Object.)

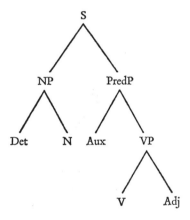

(E.g. *John became rich* by rules (i), (ii) second line, (iii), (iv) second line.)

32

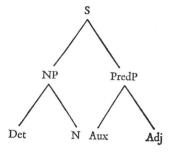

(E.g. *John was clever* by rules (i), (ii) third line, (iii).)

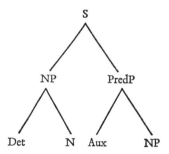

(E.g. *John was a politician* by rules (i), (ii) fourth line, (iii) twice.)

In this chapter I have shown that simple constituent structure rules – proper phrase-structure rules – are used to define a small, finite set of underlying phrase-markers. Transformations apply to one or more of these five phrase-markers to generate any of the infinite set of sentences of *L*. The PS-rules provide implicit definitions of the basic syntactic notions of 'Subject', 'Predicate' and 'Object': fundamental inter-constituent relationships are implied by these concepts, and they have to be defined so that the semantic component can make reference to them in amalgamating the meanings of lexical items.

Certain details of the nature and use of phrase-structure rules are still to be explored: in the following chapter I will discuss the construction of *derivations* using these rules, and also the *category symbols* in terms of which the rules are stated.

Exercises and topics for discussion

1. Draw labelled tree-diagrams for the underlying structures of the following sentences:

> (a) John will finish the job.
> (b) The students became revolutionaries.
> (c) The workers became sceptical.
> (d) He may be a spy.

2. Provide unlabelled tree-diagrams to show hierarchical organization in the *surface structures* of the following sentences:

> (a) She said that she would eat her words.
> (b) Three old men appeared on the screen.
> (c) I met a man who had visited Singapore.
> (d) Naturally, I shall visit them often.

3. Are the italicized words in the following sentences adjectives? Explain the criteria which this book has already provided for deciding on this question, and suggest some additional criteria:

> (a) *Every* man must do his duty.
> (b) We had *some* great movies in those days.
> (c) *Many* people dislike hard work.
> (d) The *two* remaining players fell asleep.

4. What is 'parsing'? To what technique(s) in TG does it correspond?
5. In your supplementary reading, find out as much as you can about the formal definition of phrase-structure grammar. In particular, distinguish the properties of context-free and context-sensitive PSGs.

four

Constituent Structure: Categories and Derivations

For cónvenience of reference, here again are the four phrase-structure rules which, according to the previous chapter, the base of the syntax must contain:

(i) S → NP + PredP

(ii) PredP → Aux + $\begin{Bmatrix} V \\ VP \\ Adj \\ NP \end{Bmatrix}$

(iii) NP → Det + N

(iv) VP → V + $\begin{Bmatrix} NP \\ Adj \end{Bmatrix}$

We now turn our attention to the symbols which are manipulated by these rules. There are nine symbols: *S*, *PredP*, *NP*, *VP*, *N*, *V*, *Adj*, *Det* and *Aux*. All except *S* are names for types of constituents, for constituent parts of higher-level units. *S* is called the *initial symbol* of the grammar – the force of the term 'initial' will become obvious when we consider derivational processes in the latter half of this chapter: it is the symbol with which every derivation begins. It stands for the class of objects – underlying P-markers – which the PSG defines. Note that *S* does not stand for 'sentence': 'sentence' is a general term for one of the class of objects which the grammar as a whole, and not just the phrase-structure section, defines. A sentence may consist of one *S* or of more than one.

The two immediate constituents of *S* are *NP* and *PredP*. The division is into the constituents which perform the syntactic functions of Subject and Predicate respectively, and we see that these constituents have rather different status. The exponent of the Subject must be an *NP* – and, conversely, the *NP* immediately dominated by *S* must be the Subject. For this reason, it would be redundant to introduce the term 'Subject' into the rules. (Notice the distinction drawn here between a syntactic *function*, e.g. Subject, and a syntactic *category*, a class of formatives. A category is said to be the *exponent* of a function: *NP* is the exponent of, or 'expounds', the function Subject.) Now the Predicate has four alternative exponents, so we cannot use the notational shorthand of category-for-function as we did for Subject. We need what is called an *auxiliary symbol* (which is nothing to do with the element *Aux*): a cover-term for the four alternative predicating constituents. We might choose some arbitrary label, say 'X', but for mnemonic convenience *Predicate-Phrase* seems preferable. *VP* also is an auxiliary symbol: it subsumes two choices of construction based on *V*. *NP* is a class of phrases based on *N*, but it is unlike *VP* in that there is no choice: the symbol *N* must always occur, accompanied by *Det*.

    N, V, Adj, Det and *Aux* are known as *terminal symbols*: the last line of a derivation, the end-points of the bottom branches in a tree, are made up of a selection from this set of symbols. These are symbols which cannot be analysed further in syntax by a constituent structure technique: there can be no syntactic branching below these symbols. This is not to say that terminal symbols are not subject to further analysis, only that no analysis of terminal symbols into constituent segments has any bearing on the syntax of the strings containing them.

    N, V and *Adj* on the one hand, and *Det* and *Aux* on the other, are quite different kinds of element, and make distinct (and complementary) contributions to the meanings of sentences. *N, V* and *Adj* are *lexical category symbols*. Through them, 'dictionary meanings' enter sentences. As each underlying string contains a Subject and a Predicate, implying a topic and a comment on that topic, so each such string must contain at least two occurrences of a lexical category symbol: *N* and *V*, *N* and *N*, *N* and *Adj*, *N*, *V* and *N* or *N*, *V* and *Adj*. Through the device of predication, a simple proposition is formed from the semantic materials introduced by lexical items. Each of the symbols marks a class of lexical items which are privileged to occur in that part of constituent structure pinpointed by the category symbol. *Det* and *Aux*, however, are not symbols for classes of lexical items, nor do they introduce dictionary meanings. They are *deictic* formatives, whose role is to 'locate' a proposition in relation to the whole scheme of different contexts in which one might use it. Given a proposition about a black cat, one must be guided

36

into an 'orientation' relative to it. In examples (24)–(26) this proposition was located in past time: tense is a deictic property of the formative *Aux*. Again, the deictic features of *Det* – which was expressed in (24)–(26) as *the* – link the proposition to a particularly specified cat, not any cat or cats in general. Another deictic contrast is carried by the formatives *this* and *that* (which are surface structure realizations of one dimension of *Det*): '*N* near the speaker' versus '*N* distant from the speaker'. *Det* and *Aux* are discussed in detail in Chapter 6; for the moment, we need to know only their general purpose: to 'place' a proposition in relation to an extra-linguistic context, using as notional points of reference the space-time-person dimensions of the situation of utterance.

Let us return to *N*, *V* and *Adj*. These categories are obviously a distillation, in the services of a formalized PSG, of the traditional classification of words into 'parts of speech' or 'word-classes'. The need for lexical categorization arises from a pressure external to vocabulary: the necessity that, in syntax, all lexical items should not have identical distributional privileges – if the parts of speech were not mutually exclusive, any random string of lexical items would be as grammatical as any other. So lexical categorization, though expressed in the organization of the vocabulary, is essentially a syntactic mechanism. It has been said that lexical categorization 'simplifies the syntax' and it is very easy to see that this is so. The number of rules in syntax decreases in proportion to the sophistication of the system of lexical classification, especially the generality of the categories. It is largely due to the power of generalization of *N*, *V* and *Adj* that we are able to reduce our base PSG to just four rules. The rules apply to large categories of the vocabulary, and so are much more economical than rules which apply to individual cases.

Traditional grammar has left us with a rich descriptive terminology for lexical categories, and a host of problems in its application. The most common terms (those usually given, for example, in pedagogic grammars of European languages) include *noun, pronoun, article, adjective, verb, adverb, preposition, conjunction,* and *interjection.* The chief obstacle to exploring the rationale and utility of these categories is the elusiveness of the usual criteria for defining them. A noun is said to be 'the name of a person, place or thing' while an adjective symbolizes a 'quality' and a verb 'a state, process or action'. These are 'notional' or 'referential' criteria: that is, they attempt to put lexical items into sets according to the types of conceptual signification they manifest, the kinds of concept they designate. It is not at all obvious that such semantic criteria ought to be invoked in order to achieve what is essentially a syntactic classification. But, lacking a firm distinction between syntax and semantics, it is very difficult to find a formal proof or disproof of the validity of such criteria. What we can show, however, is that notional criteria of this kind, applied in the way they usually are, lead to an inconsistent and incomplete analysis. If nouns denote objects, *rug* is a noun; if adjectives denote qualities, then *beautiful* is an adjective; if verbs denote actions and processes, then *strike* and *develop* are verbs. So far, so good. But *honesty* and *beauty* would presumably be called qualities, yet are nouns; likewise, *acclimatization* is a process, *pursuit* and *betrayal* actions, but one would not usually call them verbs. Pairs like *pursue/pursuit, strong/strength, beauty/beautiful, develop/development* call the whole procedure into question. No semantic description, based on referential or any other similar principles, could reasonably differentiate the members of these pairs, and yet it is obvious that a syntactic account must separate them as belonging to different parts of speech. If we try this referential criterion on more extensive materials, we simply uncover greater numbers of cases where the semantic tests are inconclusive. Also, we discover that the basic referential tests are not applicable to (and are not usually applied to) certain areas of the vocabulary. Whereas it is fairly easy to designate many nouns, verbs and adjectives as 'things', 'actions', 'qualities', etc., appropriate notional labels for other types of lexical items are extremely difficult to formulate: what are we to call *and, to, but, whereas, will, etc., the, if, in so far as, thus, since, not, so, furthermore*? It seems very likely that some of these words should not be categorized at all, or, if they are put into classes, certainly not put into classes defined by referential standards.

Despairing of the possibility of making the referential criteria work, and doubting their appropriateness anyway, modern linguists abandoned this approach and sought more workable criteria. They decided that lexical items should be sorted into categories on the basis of *distributional* evidence. So, for instance, a class 'noun' might be set up, not in terms of the semantic properties of its members, but on the basis of what places its members could occupy in syntactic structure. A lexical item would be called a noun if it shared a position or positions within linguistic structure in common with other items similarly labelled.

The pioneer of the distributional approach was Charles Carpenter Fries, whose book *The Structure of English*, published in 1952, illustrated at length a distributional technique for determining the parts of speech. His method was to construct a number of syntactic 'test frames', simple sentences with one word missing; a lexical category comprised all the words which could be inserted in the empty 'slot'. Thus, his frame

The ————— was good

would reveal a large class of words including *coffee, book, table, meal, play, programme, house, car,* etc. One problem with this method is that, because all words except one are specified, semantic compatibility as well as syntactic well-formedness is tested. That is to say, the semantic characteristics of the other words in the frame, as well as the syntactic properties of the frame itself, may place restrictions on what words may go into the 'slot'. It is notable that the last word in the above frame is an extremely vague all-purpose adjective. If the frame chosen were, for instance,

The ———— was loud

many nouns would be rejected: *coffee, book, table,* etc., even though these are nouns and the empty position in the frame represents a position in which nouns can be inserted. The point is that a really effective frame would be very general:

Det ———— PredP

If we use a frame of this generality we are doing something different from what Fries appears to be doing. His 'frames' test the acceptability of specific lexical items in certain positions in strings of other specific lexical items. But we have seen that a particular place within a string is *not* defined by reference to the actual words which form its context; that a structural position is characterized by the form of the phrase-marker associated with the string. So in the following diagram the position *N* is defined not by the 'horizontal' relations within the string, but by the 'vertical' route back through the tree to *S*:

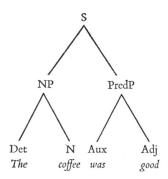

Therefore the 'frame' method of lexical categorization is a (potentially misleading) shorthand for a more realistic technique: lexical categories are defined primarily by reference to the syntactic functions which their members can perform – for it is syntactic function, remember, which the geometry of branching represents. So the defining characteristic of the noun is that it is (among other things) the exponent of the functions 'Subject' and 'Object'.

Syntactic function is the chief, but not sole, criterion of lexical category. As we shall see, there are supplementary morphological and transformational criteria.

Our base PSG defines a smaller set of categories than traditional grammar provides: *N, V, Adj, Det* and *Aux*. Of these, *N, V* and *Adj* are lexical category symbols and thus the same kind of thing as traditional grammar attempts to define in its 'parts of speech'. *Det* and *Aux* are *not* categories, and I would give the special caution that they are *not* to be equated with the surface structure classes of articles (*the, a,* etc.) and auxiliary verbs (*may, will, be,* etc.) – although such words are related to *Det* and *Aux* by transformation. So far I have not mentioned certain types of word and morpheme for most of which traditional grammar has attempted to find homes among the parts of speech: prepositions, conjunctions, particles, inflexions, and, perhaps the most striking omission, adverbs. All of these 'classes' are features of surface structure: their members are derived transformationally from underlying forms given by the base of the grammar. Most of them are accounted for in the course of the description of English transformations later in this book; as just one illustration for the time being, take this sentence:

(60) He said that he intended to sell his house.

That and *to* are among the forms which our grammar has so far neglected. Now the sentence seems to have this structure (here simplified):

(i)

(ii)

(iii)

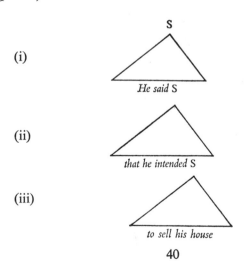

40

(Where details of the internal structure of trees are irrelevant to the point at issue, they are conventionally omitted in diagrams, plain triangles being used instead of regularly branching trees.)

The underlying structure of (60) consists of three P-markers, the first two of which have non-particularized *NP*s in the Object positions; the strings concerned might be represented informally as (i) *He said NP*, (ii) *He intended NP*, (iii) *He sold his house*. The unspecified Objects in (i) and (ii) are expounded by the whole strings (ii) and (iii) respectively. These are 'embedded' strings which have been inserted transformationally, with some modification to their constituent structure. One modification is the insertion of *that* and *to* in appropriate positions: these words do not 'mean' anything – meaning is already established, in underlying structure – and in surface structure they indicate no more than that certain specific transformations have been applied. To relate them to deep structure categories would be to aggrandize their completely mechanical functions. By similar arguments, other words which are introduced by transformations are excluded from the scheme of basic lexical categories.

We can now return to *N*, *V* and *Adj*. The words that these categories contain are manifestly essential to deep structure since they have fundamental semantic contributions to make to sentences. They are differentiated from one another by distinct syntactic functions and by secondary, transformational and morphological, factors. *N* is the sole exponent of underlying Subject (see rules (i) and (iii), p. 35); although *V* often appears as a superficial Subject (*His driving frightens me*), it can do so only after a 'nominalizing' transformation has been applied (see Ch. 11). *Via* an *NP*, *N* is one exponent of Predicate also (see rule (ii)). *V* and *Adj* are exponents of Predicate. They are distinguished from *N* by their non-appearance as Subject, and from each other by transformational and inflexional idiosyncrasies. Thus, *Adj* can be placed in front of nouns (*the black cat*); only some *V*s have this privilege, and then only with morphological alteration (*pouring rain, mashed potato*). Within the Predicate Phrase, *V*s are inflected for tense, but *Adj*s and *N*s cannot be. *Adj* can be inflected for comparative and superlative degrees (*smaller, smallest*), a facility which is not shared by *N* and *V*. There are also features of non-inflexional morphology which identify some items as belonging to particular lexical categories; for example:

41

N	V	Adj
perseverance	persevere	perseverant
existence	exist	existent
presence	present	present
automation	automate	automatic
acclimatization	acclimatize	
energy	energize	energetic
noisiness		noisy
sleepiness	sleep	sleepy
happiness		happy
driver	drive	
employee	employ	
symbolism	symbolize	symbolic

But these features are found only in a small section of the vocabulary, and thus are of limited usefulness in identifying lexical category. However, they have a certain importance: most of the nouns listed above do not inflect for plural or for possessive case, but are nevertheless marked as nouns by their derivational suffixes *-ence*, *-ness*, etc.

It will have been noticed that adverbs have been excluded from the basic lexical categories, although they are a standard part of traditional grammar. There is no doubt that adverbs and adverbials provide a useful generalization for a range of superficial constituents which can be used to restrict the meaning of a Predicate where the *PredP* contains a verb:

(61)   John eats fish *regularly*.
(62)   The visitor left *when he had finished his drink*.
(63)   I'll return *soon*.
(64)   Humpty-Dumpty sat *on a wall*.

But it is extremely difficult to provide a common deep structure origin for all these elements. Their morphological heterogeneity alone suggests a variety of transformational histories. And the apparently simple job of revising our base PSG (i)–(iv) turns out to be a very difficult enterprise. On the face of it, accommodating an extra category symbol *Adv* entails no more than increasing the 'depth' of the tree-diagram by admitting one more division into the branches:

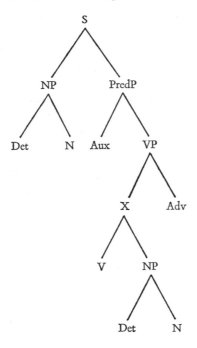

(47)   The children ate the apples noisily.

But in practice, as you will discover when you tackle exercise 3 (p. 48), there are considerable mechanical problems in the way of justifying such phrase-markers and ensuring their consistency from one type of underlying string to another. Are we to permit three branches from one node? If not, we have to resort to auxiliary symbols: but what sort of constituent is 'X'? Of course, these could be regarded as *merely* mechanical problems; but the fact that any solution to them changes the style of tree-diagrams radically suggests that they are not 'merely' mechanical problems, but problems of principle and of fundamental design.

Even more worrying is the fact that the introduction of an extra basic category 'adverb', and with it the addition of an extra path through the branches and hence of another basic syntactic function, substantially increases the complexity of our very simple grammar. At present, the grammar is based on the single notion of 'predication'. It seems undesirable to add a new one of 'adverbial modification', especially since this function is, for the majority of sentences, perfectly optional. (An exception would be *He was lying on the floor*, which does not make sense – at least, not the intended sense of *lying* – without the prepositional phrase.) Even if adverbial modification were a distinctive function, it would not be essential. And there is some evidence that it is not even distinctive. If, in (47), it is predicated of the children that they ate the apples noisily, by implication it is also predicated of their eating that it was noisy. I am suggesting that, in cases like (47) at least, the adverb is the surface structure expression of a second predicate: that such a sentence contains two instances of the relation 'predication' – two underlying P-markers, two *S*s – and thus is complex. Possibly a derivation somewhat as follows is called for:

Underlying string A: *The children ate the apples.*
Underlying string B: *NP was noisy.*
(Both of these strings imply properly formed P-markers generated by our PSG (i)–(iv).)

Transformation: nominalize A to give C: *The children's eating of the apples.*
Transformation: embed C within B at the *NP* to give D: *The children's eating of the apples was noisy.*
(We should not object that D is an 'unlikely sentence': it is simply a transitional string formed to allow us to pass along a particular derivational route; it is not suggested that D is formed *as a sentence.*)

Transformation: reform D to give E (= (47)): *The children ate the apples noisily.*

Admittedly, this procedure is inelegant: to some people, it may seem a ludicrously involved strategy. But transformational rules are inevitably complicated; and because they are hidden away beneath the surface of sentences, they may appear unnatural. The above processes are not untypical, in their complexity and unfamiliarity, of many other transformational operations which are perfectly well motivated. The benefits from having such operations are substantial: (a) they simplify the base PSG; (b) they provide a formal explanation of relationships between sentences, and between constituents, which would otherwise remain obscure. For example, one important observation on a whole section of the vocabulary is made possible by the above scheme. In English, 'descriptive adjectives' and 'manner adverbs' are morphologically related, and obviously semantically related too: *noisy/noisily, happy/happily, pretty/prettily, perfect/ perfectly,* etc. By treating manner adverbs as surface realizations of descriptive adjectives, as above, we provide a formal presentation of these relationships. Hopefully, we may in time be able to provide transformational explanations for other types of adverbial, so preserving the simplicity of the base component of the syntax.

44

I will conclude this chapter with a discussion of a topic which has been mentioned in passing several times: the notion of *derivation*. Derivation is the process in which the linguist uses the rules of the grammar to assign structural descriptions to sentences. He begins with the initial symbol of the grammar *S*, and, applying linguistic rules one at a time, progresses, by as many steps as are necessary, to a derived string which expresses the surface structure of a sentence. By taking note of which rules are used, and in what order, we can determine the underlying phrase-marker(s), the superficial phrase-marker, and the intervening transformational history, of a sentence. At the moment we do not have sufficient information to take us right through a derivation, only to the stage of the underlying P-marker. The complete process may be shown diagrammatically:

S (one or more)
.
.
.
n applications of PS-rules
.
.
.
Underlying string(s)
.
.
.
m applications of T-rules
.
.
.
Derived or superficial string

A derivation is usually set out as a sequence of lines. Each line is formed by applying one and only one rule to a symbol in the preceding line. The first line is *S*, and to this we must apply PS-rule (i) to form line (2):

(1) S
(2) NP + PredP   (by rule (i), $S \rightarrow NP + PredP$)

Now that we see rules being applied to symbols in strings, we can give a new interpretation to the single arrow ' $\rightarrow$ '. On p. 30 above I said that ' $\rightarrow$ ' means 'consists of'. In the present context, the arrow can be seen as an instruction to 'rewrite *S* as *NP + PredP*' – in formal terms, 'rewrite *A* as *X* followed by *Y*'. This is why phrase-structure

rules are often called 'rewriting rules'. Alternatively, we could say
that rule (i) 'expands' *S* as *NP* followed by *PredP*.

There are two directions we might take after line (2). We can either
apply rule (ii), rewriting the symbol *PredP*, or (iii), expanding *NP*.
As a pure convenience, we choose to rewrite *NP*, since moving from
left to right assists the reading of derivations:

(3) $Det + N + PredP$ (by rule (iii), $NP \rightarrow Det + N$)

With *PredP*, there is a substantive, and not merely procedural,
choice. Which line of rule (ii) we choose determines what type of
derived string we can arrive at. Taking one possibility, the second line
of (ii), we have

(4) $Det + N + Aux + VP$

Only *VP* in line (4) can be expanded, since the other three symbols
are terminal. Choosing the first line of (iv) we construct

(5) $Det + N + Aux + V + NP$

Now rule (iii) has to be applied a second time:

(6) $Det + N + Aux + V + Det + N$

This is as far as the rewriting rules can take us, for all the symbols in
the line are now terminal. We need now to substitute selected lexical
items for the category symbols *N* (twice) and *V*, and to replace *Det*
and *Aux* with selected deictic features. (We will see in the next two
chapters that this lexical and deictic 'fleshing-out' of terminal
symbols calls for T-rules.) Finally, the lexically and deictically
interpreted string must be submitted to whatever further transformational processing is necessary to pass from underlying to
superficial structure. Here, then, is an example of a derivation in as
much detail as the discussion up to this point will allow:

(1) S
(2) $NP + PredP$ (by rule (i))
(3) $Det + N + PredP$ (by rule (iii))
(4) $Det + N + Aux + VP$ (by rule (ii), second line)
(5) $Det + N + Aux + V + NP$ (by rule (iv), first line)
(6) $Det + N + Aux + V + Det + N$ (by rule (iii))
(7) $Det + John + Aux + eat + Det + apples$ (lexical insertion)
(8)–(9) *John* + Past + *eat* + *the* + *apples*   (*Det* and *Aux* specified)
(10) *John* + *eat* + Past + *the* + *apples*   (affix-shifting, above, p. 17)

(11) *John ate the apples*   (morphological rules pro-
                                              duce surface structure)

Or (1)–(9) as above, then

(10) Past + *John* + *eat* + *the* + *apples*   (*Aux* moved to beginning of sentence for question)

(11) Past + *do* + *John* + *eat* + *the* + *apples*   (*do* inserted to carry Past)

(12) *Do* + Past + *John* + *eat* + *the* + *apples*   (affix-shifting, above, p. 17)

(13) *Did John eat the apples*   (surface structure; phonology will convert to phonemes and introduce rising intonation for question at (14))

(14) *Did John eat the apples?*

Such a derivation as the above gives a great deal of information about the syntactic structure of the target sentence. On the basis of the derivation, we can draw trees for underlying, intermediate and superficial structures. The further one moves down the derivational process, the more explicit is the derivation compared with any tree that could be drawn for an equivalent stage. A particular advantage over trees of the fully-written-out derivation in its later stages is that it shows the *order* in which T-rules are applied, a particularly crucial fact which it is impossible to retrieve from tree-diagram representations of superficial P-markers. In subsequent chapters, many examples of the importance of the order of transformational processes will be encountered.

Finally, I must reiterate that a derivation recapitulates the stages a grammarian goes through as he constructs a structural description. It does *not* list the operations a speaker performs in constructing a sentence. Nothing whatever is known about the psychology of sentence-construction. And in any case, a derivation could not conceivably serve as a psycholinguistic model of sentence-production. Notice, for instance, that the general syntactic character of the sentence is accounted for (lines (1)–(6)) *before* lexical items are inserted (line (7)). To regard the derivation as a model of sentence production would be tantamount to saying that a speaker decides on the overall shape of a sentence before he decides what the sentence is about: this is obviously a nonsensical model for sentence production – however, it is not designed to model sentence production.

Exercises and topics for discussion

1. Look at C. C. Fries's *The Structure of English* and provide a critical discussion of his method of lexical categorization.

2. Find out as much as you can about the history of the conventional lexical categories (parts of speech) within the European linguistic tradition.

3. Draw tree-diagrams, using the symbols provided so far plus any others you may need to invent, for all possible analyses of the following sentences:

  (a) The children ate noisily.
  (b) The children ate the apples noisily.

Discuss the advantages and disadvantages of the various tree structures which you produce for (b).

4. Consider the following sets of sentences and draw tentative conclusions about the status of the italicized words and phrases:

  (i) (a) Seymour cut the salami *with a knife.*
      (b) Seymour used a knife to cut the salami.
      (c) Seymour used a knife. Seymour cut the salami.
  (ii) (a) The child travelled *with the nurse.*
      (b) The child and the nurse travelled together.
      (c) The child travelled. The nurse travelled.
  (iii) (a) John visited Russia *with a model of the factory.*
      (b) John visited Russia. John took a model. The model depicted the factory.

5. Explain the following variety of usage in relation to a single formal category of rules: 'branching rules', 'phrase-structure rules', 'rewriting rules', 'constituent structure rules'. What differences of emphasis are reflected in this terminology?

6. Write out derivations, and draw labelled tree-diagrams, for the underlying strings of the following sentences:

  (a) These people are demonstrators.
  (b) The boys were kicking a football.
  (c) The man who won the pools went wild.
  (d) John wants Helen to leave.

7. What is a 'linguistic rule'?

five

Lexical Interpretation

In this and the following chapter we focus on two stages in derivation which occur immediately after the PSG has generated an underlying string. These were represented in lines (7) and (8)–(9) in our sample derivation of the previous chapter. Line (6) showed the output of the PSG as a string of abstract syntactic symbols, some lexical and some deictic:

Det + N + Aux + V + Det + N

Line (7) substitutes real lexical items for *N* and *V*, and thus relates the string to a specific topic of discourse:

Det + *John* + Aux + *eat* + Det + *apple*

Lines (8)–(9), which were conflated in the sample derivation, introduce precise realizations of *Det* and *Aux*. The effect of these substitutions is to place the topic of discourse in a setting: to 'orientate' the speaker and hearer, and their time and place of discourse, in relation to a setting relevant to the statement:

John + Past + *eat* + *the* + *apples*

In a full derivation, each of these two stages would occupy several lines, not just the one given for the lexical process and the two allowed for the specification of *Det* and *Aux*. The sample derivation shows only the general nature of what happens and – but this is extremely important – the fact that lexical interpretation occurs *before* the two 'deictic' symbols are replaced.

Line (6) describes underlying syntactic structure in the most general terms possible. It arises from the application of a particular set of rules which, in their first formulation in this book, were linked with the following examples:

(48)   The children ate the apples.
(50)   This truck weighs three tons.
(51)   John became a politician.

(50) and (51) differ from (48) in that only (48) can be turned into the passive. Our grammar does not yet provide a way of distinguishing these two different types of construction: *VP*-dominated *NP*s which are Objects and *VP*-dominated *NP*s which are not Objects. Both receive the same syntactic representation – line (6); line (7) allows us to distinguish them, but only inexplicitly and inefficiently, by listing the sentences concerned. We have no mode of representation which is less general than (6) and more general than (7).

Again, line (6) does not prevent the generation of large numbers of ungrammatical sentences. The following would all receive the representation (6):

(65)   *The children ate the frankness.
(66)   *This truck weighs a politician.
(67)   *John became a truck.
(68)   *Stones eat bread.
(69)   *The children sleep apples.

Other terminal strings of our PSG admit similarly ill-formed sentences. The string $Det + N + Aux + V$ will yield such unacceptable sentences as

(70)   *He wants.
(71)   *These writers own.

The problem seems to be that our symbols N, V (and, in fact, *Adj*) are too inclusive. Defining broad generalities within the vocabulary as a whole, they miss distinctions at a lower level of generalization. *Wants* in (70) is a verb, but additionally it is a verb that needs to be followed by an Object – unlike *sleep*, which is misused in (69) because it must not be followed by an Object. At our high level of categorization, *weigh* and *become* ((50) and (51)) are verbs too, but (unlike *want*) must not be used in passive constructions. Then, there are two senses of *weigh* (cf. *grow*): the one which has been illustrated already, and the other which *can* be used in passives:

(72)   The politician was weighed by his doctor.

The ungrammaticalness of (66) is not related to its passivizability, but to the fact that the Subject of the sentence is not an animate, human, noun. Turning back to (65), we notice that the Object of *ate* should be concrete rather than (as *frankness* is) abstract; moreover, it should be chosen from that section of the lexicon which denotes foodstuffs. In the case of (68), *eat* should have an animate but not necessarily, as with (66), human, Subject.

It is fairly clear that we have here a problem in sub-categorization: that our theory of lexical categories must be accompanied by a description of the sub-categories within those major classes. This is necessary because not all members of the same lexical category have the same distributional privileges. In fact, there are of course distributional sub-regularities: that is to say, the privileges of members are not wholly idiosyncratic, but to a certain degree systematic. So we are going to find lexical items grouping themselves together in regularly differentiated ways within the major class.

One way of accounting for sub-category differences, and of ensuring that words from inappropriate lexical sub-categories are not inserted into strings of particular constituent structures, would be to expand the base PSG so that it contained sub-category symbols developed from category symbols. This solution was adopted in early versions of TG. For instance, we might have this rule in addition to (i)–(iv):

$$V \rightarrow \begin{Bmatrix} V_{tr} \\ V_{intr} \end{Bmatrix} \quad \text{'A verb may be either transitive or intransitive.'}$$

The first observation we might make on this rule is that it is redundant, since the grammar already includes facilities for generating both strings containing an Object-*NP* and strings without an Object-*NP*. In the following terminal strings, the differentiated sub-category symbols only duplicate information which can be inferred from their contexts anyway:

$$\text{Det} + \text{N} + \text{Aux} + V_{intr}$$
$$\text{Det} + \text{N} + \text{Aux} + V_{tr} + \text{Det} + \text{N}$$

(And the same information still has to be given in the lexicon for each separate V; three representations of the same information seems wasteful.)

Second, the rule as stated is not delicate enough. As we have seen, there are 'transitive' verbs which cannot be used in passive constructions (*become*, *weigh* in (50)); verbs which can be used in passive constructions but only if the underlying Subject is animate and human (*weigh* in (72)). There are also transitive verbs of which the Object can be deleted, and which clearly belong to a different sub-category from straight transitives:

(73)   John eats spaghetti.

(74)   John eats.

Further enlarging our base PSG to cover these facts, we might produce rules like the following:

(a) $V \rightarrow \begin{Bmatrix} V_{tr} \\ V_{intr} \end{Bmatrix}$

(b) $V_{tr} \rightarrow \begin{Bmatrix} V_{tr} - \text{pass} \\ V_{tr} - \text{non-pass} \end{Bmatrix}$

(c) $V_{tr} - \text{pass} \rightarrow \begin{Bmatrix} V_{tr} - \text{pass} - \text{Object-deletion} \\ V_{tr} - \text{pass} - \text{non-Object-deletion} \\ V_{tr} - \text{pass} - \text{human Subject} \\ V_{tr} - \text{pass} - \text{human or non-human Subject} \end{Bmatrix}$

Presumably we are still only scratching the surface of verb sub-categorization: other facts need representing in yet more supplementary rules, each subordinate rule covering fewer and fewer cases. Is there any natural end to this proliferation? And since the dictionary in any case has to give all this information again, we are committing ourselves to a very uneconomical grammar.

Another objection to this device of sub-categorization rules in the base PSG is that the logical relationships between sub-categories quickly become obscure. In rule (c) above, the first and second lines are related, as are lines three and four, but there seems to be no good reason for bracketing together the top two with the bottom two. The formal conventions for presenting PS-rules dictate this bracketing, and in doing so perhaps they create a false expectation of logical tidiness.

Note that *eat* belongs to the first and the fourth of the sub-categories defined by rule (c); *weigh* as in (72) to both the second and the third. These are simple instances of a phenomenon known as *cross-classification* which has to be taken account of in any taxonomic system: *weigh* and *eat* are things which belong to a certain category if you look at them from one perspective, another category when seen from a different angle. To take a non-linguistic example, from one point of view *homo sapiens* is an air-breathing kind of animal; from another, an animal which bears its young in a uterus. Breathing air and bearing young inside a womb are both defining characteristics of man, but are unrelated: compare birds (egg-laying, air-breathing) and fish (egg-laying, non-air-breathing). Again, birds have two legs and fly, men have two legs but don't fly, insects lay eggs and fly but have more than two legs; dogs and cats have more than two legs but don't fly, and bear their young in the uterus. These defining features multiply to yield an enormous number of randomly related and partially overlapping sub-categories which it becomes progressively more difficult and less reasonable to sort into a systematic taxonomic scheme.

The solution to this logical problem is to 'invert' it: instead of regarding the *sub-categories* as potentially systematic, we view the set of defining *features* which relate to the superordinate category of objects as systematic. So an object (e.g. a lexical item) can be presented not as a member of a sub-category but as a bundle of *distinctive features*, each one relating to some specific dimension of the overall classificatory scheme. These classifying dimensions may relate one to another in some ordered way, but since the features they yield may be put together in many different 'mixes', it would obscure the underlying system if an attempt were made to relate the individual objects by way of sub-categorization.

Where the objects to be classified are linguistic – lexical items, in this case – the effect of this decision is to shift the burden of 'sub-classification' to the lexicon. In the lexicon, each item will be identified as (a) a member of a superordinate lexical category; (b) a set of syntactic and semantic features sufficient to specify the distinctive properties of that item as against all other items; (c) a set of phonological features which give the lexical item a distinctive 'spelling'. It is the set (b) of features which concerns us here. As yet, there are many things we do not know about the representation of lexical items: we cannot determine the exact boundary between syntactic and semantic features, and we do not have any idea what range of syntactic and semantic features is available in natural languages in general or in any particular language. So distinctive features can be shown only in a very crude way.

Bearing these present uncertainties in mind, let us examine some hypothetical representations for four verbs which have been discussed above. The dictionary entries will be required to specify such information as the following; note that square brackets are used to enclose features and sets of features:

$$
eat \begin{bmatrix} +V \\ +\underline{\quad}NP \\ +\underline{\quad}[+Concrete] \\ +\underline{\quad}[+Foodstuff] \\ Opt.\ delete\ \underline{\quad}NP \\ +Pass \\ +[+Animate]\underline{\quad} \\ \cdot \\ \cdot \\ \cdot \\ +F_n \end{bmatrix}
\qquad
sleep \begin{bmatrix} +V \\ -\underline{\quad}NP \\ +[+Animate]\underline{\quad} \\ \cdot \\ \cdot \\ \cdot \\ +F_n \end{bmatrix}
$$

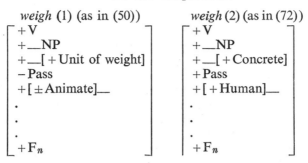

weigh (1) (as in (50))

$$\begin{bmatrix} + V \\ + \_\_NP \\ + \_\_[+ Unit\ of\ weight] \\ - Pass \\ + [\pm Animate] \_\_ \\ . \\ . \\ . \\ + F_n \end{bmatrix}$$

weigh (2) (as in (72))

$$\begin{bmatrix} + V \\ + \_\_NP \\ + \_\_[+ Concrete] \\ + Pass \\ + [+ Human] \_\_ \\ . \\ . \\ . \\ + F_n \end{bmatrix}$$

Each of these lexical items is identified as a verb: [+ V]. This means that any one of them can be substituted for the terminal symbol V (and only V) in an underlying P-marker; [+ V] implies [− N] and [− *Adj*]. Next, we learn which of these verbs can be followed by an *NP*. The notation [+ __*NP*] or [− __*NP*] gives us this information. (The lowered dash __ before *NP* indicates the position which V occupies in the string.) All except *sleep* may be followed by an *NP*. A little lower down, the feature [+ Pass] or [− Pass] indicates whether this *NP* is the Object or not: *eat* and *weigh* (2) may occur in passives, *weigh* (1) not. We are also told what kind of an *NP* may follow. *Eat* and *weigh* (2) must be followed by an *NP* denoting a [+ Concrete] object (not [− Concrete], i.e. not abstract, like *beauty*, *frankness*). The Object of *eat* is very precisely delimited: it must be foodstuff; but for *weigh* (2) the possibilities are more open: you can weigh coal or cake, but you can eat only cake. The post-verbal *NP* of *weigh* (1) is also laid down: it must be an *NP* denoting a unit of weight. One final piece of information is given on the subject of post-verbal *NP*s: that the *NP* following *eat* may optionally be deleted by a subsequent transformation.

General characteristics of pre-verbal *NP*s (i.e. Subjects) are also given. The Subject of *eat* must be [+ Animate] – stones do not eat – but it may be either [+ Human] or [− Human] – man or ape – so this feature need not be explicitly mentioned; exactly the same situation is found with *sleep*. Turning to *weigh* (1), we find that the feature [± Animate] (which means 'either [+ Animate] or [− Animate]') is assigned to the Subject position: stones, men and apes all have determinable weight. *Weigh* (2), however, is much more restricted as to the kinds of *NP*s which can precede it: only human beings can perform the operation of weighing (in the sense of 'measuring the weight of'). Notice that the entry for *weigh* (2) does not mention the feature [± Animate]: this is unnecessary as [+ Human] inevitably implies [+ Animate], and so [+ Animate] is omitted for reasons of notational economy.

(Parenthetically, we might note that, in the entry for *eat*, [+Foodstuff] similarly implies [+Concrete], yet the latter feature is specified. This redundancy is tolerated because I suspect that [+Foodstuff] is a *semantic* feature, outside the system of syntactic features which includes [+Concrete], and so [+Concrete] is, strictly speaking, not a superordinate of [+Foodstuff] as [+Animate] is of [+Human]. This is, however, sheer guesswork: the boundary between syntax and semantics is a most obscure matter.)

Finally, at the foot of each of the above hypothetical dictionary entries there appears the sequence

$$\begin{bmatrix} \cdot \\ \cdot \\ \cdot \\ +\mathbf{F}_n \end{bmatrix}$$

This notation means 'whatever semantic features are necessary to uniquely identify the given lexical item, down to the *n*th feature'. There will be a large number of such semantic features, and their job will be to distinguish particular lexical items from others with the same syntactic attributes, including near-synonyms: *eat* from *drink*, *sleep* from *laugh* and *dream*, *weigh* (2) from *measure, evaluate,* etc. At the present time, transformational-generative linguists have not yet agreed on a method of formally representing this sort of information in the lexical section of a grammar.

In the construction of a derivation, the information given in lexical entries will be utilized immediately after the line corresponding to line (6) in the sample derivation which was sketched out in the previous chapter. To put it briefly, a *lexical insertion rule* is applied to, jointly, one occurrence of a lexical symbol in a string and the set of features given in some particular lexical entry. The effect of this rule-application (which is repeated for each lexical symbol in the string) is to assign the whole set of features to the category symbol, so that, for instance, *N* in a terminal string of the PSG will become

$$\begin{bmatrix} +\mathbf{N} \\ \cdot \\ \cdot \\ \cdot \\ +\mathbf{F}_n \end{bmatrix}$$

and *V* and *Adj* in their turn will be modified accordingly. This assignment of a feature-set to a category symbol can take place only if the lexical features are compatible with other features already assigned to that string. I will now illustrate, in an informal way, how the lexical rule works.

Assume an input string (output of the base PSG, input to the lexical rule) of the following form:

$$Det + N + Aux + V + Det + N$$

This can be reduced to its essentials:

$$NP + Aux + V + NP$$

A string with this structure can accommodate at V any lexical item with the specification

$$\begin{bmatrix} +V \\ +\_NP \\ \cdot \\ \cdot \\ \cdot \\ +F_n \end{bmatrix}$$

That is, *eat, weigh* (1) or *weigh* (2) or any other of many thousands of *V*s, but not *sleep* and others of its kind. Notice that the feature-set from the lexicon is introduced by a *transformational* rule, which may be stated as follows:

$$\left. \begin{array}{l} NP + Aux + V + NP \\[2ex] \begin{bmatrix} +V \\ +\_NP \\ \cdot \\ \cdot \\ \cdot \\ +F_n \end{bmatrix} \end{array} \right\} \Rightarrow NP + Aux + \begin{bmatrix} +V \\ \cdot \\ \cdot \\ \cdot \\ +F_n \end{bmatrix} + NP$$

The contextual feature $[+\_NP]$ has done its work and now disappears from the description of the lexical item; it is thus omitted from the feature-set on the right of the double arrow.

The above rule of course prevents the generation of sentences like (69) **The children sleep apples* because the underlying string contains a post-verbal *NP* while the dictionary entry for *sleep* contains the feature $[-\_NP]$, hence the string and the lexical entry do not constitute a proper joint input to the T-rule. *Sleep* in, say, *Babies sleep* will be accounted for by a different lexical rule:

$$\left. \begin{array}{l} NP + Aux + V \\[2ex] \begin{bmatrix} +V \\ -\_NP \\ \cdot \\ \cdot \\ \cdot \\ +F_n \end{bmatrix} \end{array} \right\} \Rightarrow NP + Aux + \begin{bmatrix} +V \\ \cdot \\ \cdot \\ \cdot \\ +F_n \end{bmatrix}$$

The lexical insertion rule transfers from the dictionary to a string in a derivation all the defining features of the lexical items, which are thenceforth all present *in the string*. They include features which give the dictionary meaning of the word, and features which are relevant to further transformational processing of a string containing that word. Let us examine the immediate implications of lexical insertion in a specific case; for instance, say the lexical insertion rule has produced the following string, in which *eat* is shorthand for the complete set of its defining features:

$$\text{Det} + \text{N} + \text{Aux} + eat + \text{Det} + \text{N}$$

Referring to the lexical entry for *eat*, we find that this is, *inter alia*, an example of a string

$$\text{NP} + \text{Aux} + \begin{bmatrix} + \text{V} \\ \cdot \\ \cdot \\ \cdot \\ \text{Opt. delete \_\_NP} \\ \cdot \\ \cdot \\ \cdot \\ + \text{F}_n \end{bmatrix} + \text{NP}$$

If the Object-*NP* of this string is not lexically interpreted, the presence of the feature [Opt. delete __NP] becomes an instruction to remove *NP* by transformational deletion: (74) *John eats.* It is a similar device which prevents the generation of a passive when a string contains *weigh* (1). Returning to the example in hand, the string in which *eat* has been inserted is also an instance of the string

$$\text{NP} + \text{Aux} + \begin{bmatrix} + \text{V} \\ \cdot \\ \cdot \\ \cdot \\ +\_\_[+ \text{Concrete}] \\ +\_\_[+ \text{Foodstuff}] \\ \cdot \\ \cdot \\ \cdot \\ + \text{F}_n \end{bmatrix} + \text{NP}$$

The two features $[+\_\_[+ \text{Concrete}]]$ and $[+\_\_[+ \text{Foodstuff}]]$ serve to restrict the choice of permissible Objects of *eat*. The effect of the presence of these two features is to prevent the replacement of the

N in the Object-*NP* by any lexical item marked [– Concrete] (**John eats beauty/ frankness/ honesty*) and to ensure the insertion of an item marked [+ Foodstuff] (*John eats fish/ meat/ bread*).

We have just had an illustration of an important property of lexical interpretation: the rule for lexical insertion must make reference to features of particular items which have been inserted elsewhere in a string. The motive for this cross-reference is of course that we must prevent the generation of sentences like **John eats beauty*. Such a sentence is said to offend against the *selectional restrictions* associated with *eat* and *beauty*. Features such as [+ __[+ Concrete]] which prevent such mis-generation are called *features of selectional restriction*. Sentences (65) and (68) on p. 50 above are the result of ignoring the demands of selectional restriction. On the other hand, (69)–(71) fail to observe certain much more general principles: (69) employs an Object in conjunction with a verb marked [– __NP], while (70) and (71) neglect to provide Objects for verbs marked [+ __NP]. These sentences are said to ignore *features of strict sub-categorization* associated with the verbs. (75) manifests a sub-category error while (76) ignores a selectional restriction:

(75)   *Three tons are weighed by this truck.
       (*V* is marked [– Pass])
(76)   *This truck weighs three miles.
       (*V* is marked [+ __[+ Unit of weight]])

Because the lexical insertion T-rule is obliged to make reference to existing lexical specification (if any) so as to avoid breaking selectional restrictions, lexical interpretation cannot be carried out all at one go – simultaneously replacing all the lexical symbols which occur in an underlying string. Rather, lexical interpretation requires a cyclic sequence of transformations, each one dependent on the structure produced by the application of the preceding rule. The most successful way of ordering these transformations relative to one another seems to be 'left-to-right': so the lexical content of the Predicate is determined by that which is assigned to the Subject: *V* or *Adj* or *N* by the content of the left-most *N*, and the right-most *N* by the *V* which it follows, if it follows a *V*.

As an example, sentence (77) would be represented by the following sequence of derivational lines. (Note that, for clarity of exposition, I have here preserved contextual features which would in actuality 'disappear' when they had served their function – cf. the comment on [+ __NP] on p. 56 above.)

(77)   The accident terrified the driver.

This is an instance of the string

$$\text{Det} + \text{N} + \text{Aux} + \text{V} + \text{Det} + \text{N}$$

First, the Subject-N must be lexically interpreted:

$$\text{Det} + \begin{bmatrix} +\text{N} \\ +\text{Count} \\ -\text{Concrete} \\ \cdot \\ \cdot \\ \cdot \\ +\text{F}_n \end{bmatrix} + \text{Aux} + \text{V} + \text{Det} + \text{N}$$

Now a verb must be selected which can (but does not have to) take a [−Concrete] Subject, e.g. *terrify* or *impress* but not *eat* or *sleep*:

$$\text{Det} + \begin{bmatrix} +\text{N} \\ +\text{Count} \\ -\text{Concrete} \\ \cdot \\ \cdot \\ \cdot \\ +\text{F}_n \end{bmatrix} + \text{Aux} + \begin{bmatrix} +\text{V} \\ +\_\text{NP} \\ +\_[+\text{Animate}] \\ +\text{Pass} \\ +[\pm\text{Concrete}]\_ \\ \cdot \\ \cdot \\ \cdot \\ +\text{F}_n \end{bmatrix} + \text{Det} + \text{N}$$

The lexical specification for V is now compatible with that for the preceding N. In turn, it dictates the character of the N which follows. We know from the details of V that this N must be [+Animate], e.g. *man* or *driver* or *dog* but not *stone* or *frankness*. We also know, incidentally, that the following NP is an Object, and thus that the passive transformation may apply later in the derivation.

$$\text{Det} + \begin{bmatrix} +\text{N} \\ +\text{Count} \\ -\text{Concrete} \\ \cdot \\ \cdot \\ \cdot \\ +\text{F}_n \end{bmatrix} + \text{Aux} + \begin{bmatrix} +\text{V} \\ +\_\text{NP} \\ +\_[+\text{Animate}] \\ +\text{Pass} \\ +[\pm\text{Concrete}]\_ \\ \cdot \\ \cdot \\ \cdot \\ +\text{F}_n \end{bmatrix} + \text{Det} + \begin{bmatrix} +\text{N} \\ +\text{Count} \\ +\text{Animate} \\ \cdot \\ \cdot \\ +\text{F}_n \end{bmatrix}$$

Remember that the material in square brackets is to be understood as uniquely specifying particular lexical items – *accident*, *terrify* and *driver* from left to right. The string is now fully lexically interpreted in the sense that it has its complete stock of 'dictionary meaning'. The method of introducing the lexical material – by an ordered sequence of transformational rules – ensures that the lexical items are strung together in such a way as to avoid violations of sub-categorization rules and selectional restrictions.

Note that lexical interpretation is a purely *syntactic* process. It does no more than what I have just indicated: it locates lexical items in strings and it prevents ill-formed sequences of items. It does *not* explain how the meanings of words are amalgamated to provide the meanings of sentences: how complex 'blocks' of meaning are formed in sentences like (77), how sentence-meanings are related to 'smaller' elements of meaning like the square-bracketed feature sets given for (77), and, ultimately, to constituent elements of meaning like [+Foodstuff] and other even more specific features. These relations and processes are the subject-matter of semantic theory, and thus beyond the scope of the present book.

Exercises and topics for discussion

1. The rules for lexical insertion could be called 'context-sensitive' in that they make reference to the structural characteristics of the frames in which lexical items are inserted. On the other hand, PS-rules make no reference to context and thus could be called 'context-free' rules – *NP* is rewritten as *Det + N* in whatever circumstances it occurs. Investigate further the distinction between context-sensitive and context-free rules.

2. Find some more examples of selectional restriction features and of sub-categorization features. (The discussion in Chomsky's *Aspects of the Theory of Syntax*, pp. 75 ff., may help you.)

3. Discuss the differences between 'feature analysis' and 'category analysis', referring to non-linguistic as well as linguistic classifications.

4. Sketch out dictionary entries for the following lexical items, using the features suggested in Ch. 5 and proposing others where necessary:

cry, discover, remain, truth, wife, horse, stone, happy, large.

5. Beginning with the initial symbol *S* and proceeding as far as the techniques of Chs. 3–5 will allow you, provide derivations for each of the following sentences:

(a) The nurse weighed the patient.
(b) The actor became an alcoholic.
   (Note: there is a selection restriction between the two *N*s.)
(c) The students are intelligent.

six

Deixis: *Det* and *Aux*

Two terminal symbols of underlying phrase-markers remain uninterpreted: *Det* and *Aux*. On pp. 36–7 I indicated very informally what their function is: if lexical category symbols introduce 'dictionary meanings' into derivations, and the semantic component of the grammar – under syntactic guidance – forms these meanings into whole topics of discourse, *Det* and *Aux* serve to relate these topics to the universe of possible ways of looking at the topics: they provide a kind of 'perspective' on the propositional content of sentences.

Every utterance is made in a particular place and at a particular time, by a certain speaker to a certain audience. The deictic formatives 'orientate' them by reference to these contexts of situation. The Greek word *deixis* means 'pointing': the deictic qualities of a sentence point to its location in relation to a spatio-temporal-personal context. Take, for example, the following sentence, in which the tense of *Aux* and the meaning of the adverb join forces to achieve a temporal orientation, and the pronoun relates the topic of the sentence to a complex of in-context human participants:

(78)   We went to the seaside yesterday.

A simple case of deixis is provided by the demonstratives *this* and *that*, which distinguish degrees of proximity relative to the speaker:

(79)   This is my coat and this is yours. (E.g. picking up two coats in succession.)
(80)   This is my coat and that's yours. (Picking up one coat and pointing to another.)

More subtle differentiations of proximateness are found in personal pronoun systems: *I* (identity of speaker with a participant in the sentence's topic); *you* ('not-*I*', not proximate); *we* ('*I* and a proximate not-*I* or not-*I*s'); *they* ('not-*I* and not-*you*' – the ultimate in personal non-proximateness).

It might be thought that deictic categories are universal: that such distinctions as 'near' vs. 'far', 'today' vs. 'yesterday' vs. 'tomorrow' are unalterable in objective nature and so invariable in their linguistic presentation. In fact, there are substantial differences in deictic systems from language to language; the fact that there are, and that we find it difficult to acknowledge the possibility that there are, illustrates strikingly the truism that we codify nature in terms of the structure of our own language and find it very difficult to conceive of it any other way. For instance, our time distinctions are by no means immutable: we could divide time up into 'now' and 'not-now' (making no distinction between past and future); or 'future' and 'not-future' (making no distinction between present and past) or 'distant past', 'recent past', 'near future', 'distant future', etc. Likewise, our binary distinction of proximateness (*this/that, near/far, now/then*, etc.) is not inevitable. We could have, for instance, a distinction between 'in sight' and 'out of sight' or a more complex set of differentiations: near me/ near you/ far from me/ far from you/ far from both of us, etc. As another example, the information coded in modern English *we* is 'I and you (sg.)', 'I and you (pl.)', 'I and he', 'I and she', 'I and they'; this information could be coded differently, to make these distinctions of person overlap less. Old English had, in addition to the pronouns *ic* (I) and *wē*, a 'dual' pronoun *wit* 'I and you (sg.)' or 'I and he', contrasting with *wē* and assigning to *wē* a smaller range of meanings than are covered by its modern English equivalent. Clearly, many other possibilities are available to a system such as the personal pronouns; and this potentiality for variation is quite characteristic of other deictic dimensions.

In English, deictic information and associated meanings – such as definiteness, aspect, number, mood and so on – are conveyed by a very large variety and quantity of morphemes and morpheme-sequences in surface structure. See, for instance, the italicized words and phrases in these sentences:

(81) *Man* is mortal.
(82) *The boys* were mischievous.
(83) *The three houses* were almost demolished.
(84) *Some of my friends* live in flats.
(85) *Nearly all the children* were from underprivileged families.
(86) We *were going* to London.
(87) We *had eaten* already.
(88) You *can go* if you wish.

(89)   She *liked* to knit.
(90)   He *hit* the ball solidly.

The traditional way of handling this sort of material is to note what morphemes occur and in what sequences, to sort them into classes and attach meanings to them: so we have sub-categories of articles, cardinal and ordinal numbers, demonstratives, noun and verb inflexions, modal auxiliaries, and so on. But this technique obscures the situation, since there is no simple relationship between underlying meanings and their superficial representations – this is because *Det* and *Aux* are not categories to be split up into sub-categories, but complexes of features, some obligatory and some optional, which can be put together in various combinations which are then associated in rather idiosyncratic ways with surface structure representations.

Det and *Aux* are obligatory. That is to say, there are always some features of their underlying meanings present in sentences, even where no morpheme marks the fact in surface structure. So *Det* is present in, for example, (81); even though there is no article, the *NP* has deictic meaning: it carries an implication of universality, and the Predicate comments on *all* men. Contrast

(91)   *The man* was guilty

where the presence of *the* specifies *man* as definite, a particular man. The point is that the physically non-present morpheme 'zero' in (81) signals a meaning of *Det* just as directly as does the morpheme *the* of (91).

As a final example of this non-correspondence of deictic meanings and their superficial representations, consider this pair:

(92)   Some boys are mischievous.
(93)   Some boys were seen near the station.

(92) means 'of the class of phenomena "boys", it is true that a certain small proportion are mischievous'; (93) 'an indeterminate number of boys were seen near the station'. The *Det* of (92) contains the feature 'universality': the statement is made about boys as a general truth. Additionally, 'quantification' is assigned to the statement: it is not all boys but *some boys*, where *some* belongs to a system of proportional quantification including also *all, few, many*, etc. By contrast, the *Det* of (93) is non-universal and indefinite: here, *some* is not contrasted with *all*, etc., but is a regular plural form for the indefinite article – *a boy, some boys*. On the other hand, in a sentence like *a boy is often more aggressive than a girl*, the morpheme *a* is universalized and not simply indefinite. These facts about the meanings of the *NP*s of (92) and (93) would be quite obscured in an approach to *Det* which attempted, on the basis of materials such as those evidenced

in (81)–(85), to classify the morphemes accompanying *N* (*a, some,* etc.) and then attach meanings of *Det* to them.

So *Det* is a set of abstract syntactic features, some deictic in the sense just defined, some in a looser sense. The set is partially ordered, in that some features can be selected only if others have already been chosen; there are dependency relations among certain of the features. Another characteristic of this cluster of syntactic meanings is that some of them are obligatory while others are optional. There are two mandatory features of *Det* in respect of which every *NP* must be specified: Number and Universality. This fact can be stated in a simple rule, the rule which is applied to the symbol *Det* of an underlying string when continuing a derivation after lexical interpretation:

$$\text{Det} \rightarrow \begin{bmatrix} \text{Number} \\ \text{Universality} \end{bmatrix}$$

[Number] needs little explanation. In English, it is a binary choice, seen for example in the following pair of sentences:

(94) The train was late.
(95) The trains were late.

Binary choices are customarily symbolized in a $+/-$ notation. We will therefore say that the *Det* of (94) contains [− Plural], whereas [+Pl] is present in the *Det* of (95). Not all nouns allow free choice as between [+Pl] and [−Pl]. Notably, nouns such as *John, Susan* and *meat, water* can, in normal circumstances, be [−Pl] only; on the other hand, nouns such as *table, pen, man, tree* can be [+Pl] or [−Pl]. *Meat, water, sand,* etc., are called *mass* nouns or *non-count* nouns; *table, tree,* etc., are *count* nouns; *John, Susan,* etc., are *proper* nouns or *names*. In a feature analysis, nouns must be marked as [+Name] (*John*) or [−Count] (*meat*) or [+Count] (*tree*) in their lexical specifications in strings, and T-rules have to be applied which will select an appropriate Number in terms of the features entailed in the lexical choice. (This is one of the reasons why lexical interpretation takes place before *Det* is specified − the rules which develop features of *Det* must be able to make reference to certain features of individual nouns.) The restrictions can be stated in a pair of obligatory T-rules, one or other of which must be applied immediately after the *Det*-expanding rule above; the choice between them depends on the type of noun that has been inserted in the prior process of lexical interpretation:

$$\begin{bmatrix} \text{Number} \\ \text{Universality} \end{bmatrix} + \begin{bmatrix} +\text{N} \\ \left\{ \begin{array}{l} +\text{Name} \\ -\text{Count} \end{array} \right\} \end{bmatrix} \Rightarrow \begin{bmatrix} -\text{Pl} \\ \text{Universality} \end{bmatrix} + \begin{bmatrix} +\text{N} \\ \left\{ \begin{array}{l} +\text{Name} \\ -\text{Count} \end{array} \right\} \end{bmatrix}$$

This rule means '[Number] must be developed as [−Pl] when the accompanying noun is marked either [+Name] or [−Count]'.

The alternative rule, which must be applied if a count noun has been selected, is as follows:

$$\begin{bmatrix}\text{Number} \\ \text{Universality}\end{bmatrix} + \begin{bmatrix}+\text{N} \\ +\text{Count}\end{bmatrix} \Rightarrow \begin{bmatrix}\{\pm\text{Pl}\} \\ \text{Universality}\end{bmatrix} + \begin{bmatrix}+\text{N} \\ +\text{Count}\end{bmatrix}$$

'[Number] may be developed as either [+Pl] or [−Pl] when the accompanying noun is marked [+Count].' These rules together ensure that *Det* marks every *NP* as either singular or plural, and that only 'pluralizable' nouns are assigned a [+Pl] *Det*.

The system 'Universality' is a little more complicated. Most obviously, it accounts for sentences like *Man is mortal, All men are equal, Some boys are mischievous*, all of which have [+Universal] *NP*s. However, names and pronouns are, virtually by definition, [−Universal], since they identify specific people and things. We acknowledge this fact by the following rule:

$$\begin{bmatrix}\text{Number} \\ \text{Universality}\end{bmatrix} + \begin{bmatrix}+\text{N} \\ \begin{Bmatrix}+\text{Name} \\ +\text{Pron}\end{Bmatrix}\end{bmatrix} \Rightarrow \begin{bmatrix}\text{Number} \\ -\text{Univ}\end{bmatrix} + \begin{bmatrix}+\text{N} \\ \begin{Bmatrix}+\text{Name} \\ +\text{Pron}\end{Bmatrix}\end{bmatrix}$$

Count and non-count nouns, on the other hand, may be either [+Univ] or [−Univ]:

$$\begin{bmatrix}\text{Number} \\ \text{Universality}\end{bmatrix} + \begin{bmatrix}+\text{N} \\ \{\pm\text{Count}\}\end{bmatrix} \Rightarrow \begin{bmatrix}\text{Number} \\ \{\pm\text{Univ}\}\end{bmatrix} + \begin{bmatrix}+\text{N} \\ \{\pm\text{Count}\}\end{bmatrix}$$

Some examples of the [+Univ] state are:

(96)   *Dogs* are excellent companions.
(97)   *A cat* is a very independent animal.
(98)   *Meat* is very nutritious.

But [−Univ] is not, as it were, 'self-sufficient'; by itself it is not an adequate characterization of ordinary nouns. If a count or a non-count noun is given a *Det* containing [−Univ], the string in which it occurs is subjected to an obligatory transformation which replaces [−Univ] by either [+Definite] or [−Definite]:

$$\begin{bmatrix}\text{Number} \\ -\text{Univ}\end{bmatrix} + \begin{bmatrix}+\text{N} \\ \{\pm\text{Count}\}\end{bmatrix} \Rightarrow \begin{bmatrix}\text{Number} \\ \{\pm\text{Def}\}\end{bmatrix} + \begin{bmatrix}+\text{N} \\ \{\pm\text{Count}\}\end{bmatrix}$$

'If an *NP* containing a count noun or a non-count noun is marked [−Univ], this feature must be replaced by either Definite or Indefinite.' Examples:

(99)   *The book* was enjoyable.
(100)   *A book* has been lost.
(101)   *The books* for the course were expensive.
(102)   *Some books* fell off the shelf.

(103)   *The water* was cool.
(104)   *Some water* splashed on my face.

The systems [Number] and [Universality/Definiteness] are obligatory; they define the minimal requirements for all instances of *Det*: hence appropriate rules from among the five just given must always be applied. In addition, there are a number of optional transformations which may be applied to add further dimensions to *Det*. Prominent among them are the rules for specifying proximateness, for adding cardinal and ordinal numerals (*the three men, the third man,* respectively), and also a rather involved system which quantifies *NP*s proportionally, not numerically, giving sentences such as

(105)   *A few students* failed.
(106)   *Some people* like frogs' legs.
(107)   *Many books* are uninteresting.
(108)   *Most people* eat too much.
(109)   *All the prisoners* escaped.

These optional features are introduced by applying T-rules to strings which have been derived under the obligatory rules. To illustrate how this process works I will give the rule for introducing the optional feature [Proximateness].

$$\begin{bmatrix} \text{Number} \\ +\text{Def} \end{bmatrix} + \begin{bmatrix} +\text{N} \\ \{\pm\text{Count}\} \end{bmatrix} \Rightarrow \begin{bmatrix} \text{Number} \\ +\text{Def} \\ \{\pm\text{Prox}\} \end{bmatrix} + \begin{bmatrix} +\text{N} \\ \{\pm\text{Count}\} \end{bmatrix}$$

'Any string which contains the feature [+Def] and either a count or a non-count noun may additionally be marked as either [+Proximate] or [−Proximate].' The dependence of Proximateness on Definiteness is obvious: an *NP* which is specified as 'near' or 'far' must clearly be also 'definite'. Examples:

(110)   *This meat* is tough.
(111)   *That milk* is sour.
(112)   *These apples* are sour.
(113)   *Those apples* are sweet.

Other optional features are present in *Det*, and may be selected in various combinations for particular sentences. Chief among them are [Ordinal], [Cardinal] and [Quant]. Each of these features has a range of morphemes associated with it, but their origins are similar to, and related to, the origins of the other components of *Det* considered so far. A transformational rule is required to add an abstract feature, making reference to the existing structure of the *NP* to ensure that the feature does not jar with whatever other features the *NP* contains. For instance, [Cardinal] must be introduced in such a way that only *one* co-occurs with [−Pl], and that it co-occurs with

[– Pl] only (*one shoe* but not *one shoes) and that cardinal numbers greater than one co-occur only with [+Pl] (*two shoes* but not *two shoe). But in general, these optional features of counting and quantification mix freely with the basic deictic features, and so the rules for introducing them are relatively simple.

[Quant] is expressed in surface structure by means of a variety of morphemes and arrangements of morphemes; among them: *many apples, a few of the apples, a few apples, all these apples, many of the forty-seven apples*, etc. I mention this here only to recall an observation made on pp. 62–3 above: that the relationship between underlying abstract syntactic features of *Det* and the real morphological forms in surface structure is far from direct. *Det* is not manifested in surface structure simply by substituting a word or words for the feature-set derived by the transformational rules above, letting these morphological insertions occupy the same position in the string as was occupied by the set of features. Since the number and the positioning of the morphemes associated with *Det* is very variable – [Quant] is an extreme case – a rather complex set of *realization rules* is necessary to trace the route between feature-sets and superficial structures. Realization rules are transformational rules which substitute particular morphemes for particular sets of syntactic features. I will illustrate the workings of realization rules after describing the functions of *Det*'s sister symbol, *Aux*.

Aux appears to be an exactly parallel symbol to *Det*, one to be developed by a similar two-tier sequence of rules. Like *Det*, it is first and foremost a system of syntactic meanings rather than a set of classifiable morphemes. A full analysis would distinguish and relate these meanings, offer T-rules showing how meanings are developed and built up into complexes, and draw up realization rules to carry the meanings through into appropriate sequences of morphemes in surface structure. This analysis has not yet been undertaken, but there is plenty of informal descriptive material available on matters relevant to *Aux* (there are several books on the syntax of the English verb), out of which a feature-analysis could be constructed. Although the analysis would have much the same format as that for *Det*, the materials gathered under *Aux* are a good deal more complicated.

It seems that four obligatory features of *Aux* must be present in every utterance, and our first rule shows this fact and names the features:

$$\text{Aux} \rightarrow \begin{bmatrix} \text{Tense} \\ \text{Aspect} \\ \text{Mood} \\ \text{Voice} \end{bmatrix}$$

So in the following sentence a choice is made from each of the four systems subsumed under *Aux*:

(114) I'm baking a cake.

Tense is 'Present', Aspect 'Progressive', Mood 'Indicative' and Voice 'Active'. Compare

(115) Was she being coy?

which is Past (T), Progressive (A), Interrogative (M) and Active (V). On the other hand, (116) is Past (T), Perfect (A), Indicative (M) and Passive (V):

(116) He had been sacked by the firm.

(117) is Present (T), Momentary(?) (A), Interrogative and Permissive (M) and Active (V):

(117) May I go to London?

Let us look briefly at each of these four systems in turn, beginning with Tense. Tense, in English, is a binary choice [±Past]: a sentence is either marked as Past or not marked at all. It is better not to speak of 'Past' versus 'Present', because the two terms are not exactly complementary: while 'Past' denotes 'before-the-present-time' unequivocally, 'Present' makes no such simple reference to time. (118) below, for instance, though technically [−Past], is in fact a statement about the past and present vocation of 'I', and undoubtedly carries an assumption about his future employment: he was a teacher yesterday, is a teacher today, and believes he will be a teacher tomorrow:

(118) I am a teacher.

Again, temporal implications are carried by non-tense systems. English has no future tense, but makes reference to future time by use of modal devices (often reinforced or clarified by adverbials):

(119) I will go to London (tomorrow).
(120) I may return to France (next year).
(121) I could do it for you (next week).

Interestingly, (121) is marked [+Past], but clearly concerns future time. Thus tense does not correlate neatly with time, and Tense is not the only communicator of time. A definition of the system 'Tense' in English cannot depend exclusively on a study of the time-relations expressed by English sentences.

Aspect is interrelated with Tense, most obviously in that one particular morpheme (the -*ing* form of Progressive Aspect) can be used to express future time in English:

(122) I'm leaving for London on Tuesday.

A more important interconnection of Tense and Aspect is that Aspect characterizes the manner, duration, repetition, etc., of an action or state relative to a time-scale. (Many Aspects found in other languages, such as benefactive, causative, intensive, are not expressed in English.) Some basic aspectual contrasts in English are represented by the following sentences:

(123) I closed the door. (One action in the past.)
(124) We're going to the library. (Either a continuing action in the present, or an action in the future.)
(125) I've finished my homework. ('and can now go out to play': a completed action relevant to the present.)
(126) I had opened the door. ('before I saw who it was': a completed action with relevance to subsequent, but past, time.)
(127) I was walking down the street. (Continuous action in the past, not embracing the present.)
(118) I am a teacher. (Statement about yesterday, today and tomorrow.)
(128) Water boils at 100° Centigrade. (An 'eternal truth', as applicable now as it always was and always will be.)
(129) I had been reading *Giles Goat-Boy*. (A continuous activity up to a past point of time, when some subsequent action occurred.)

Two important Aspects in English are Progressive and Perfect. Progressive is realized as the *-ing* form of verbs – see sentences (124), (127), (129). It indicates ongoing actions or continuing states, and is combined with either [– Past] or [+ Past] Tense, depending on whether the action continues through the present (but has some foreseeable end) or stops short of present time. Contrast (124) – on one reading – with (127). As (129) attests, Progressive may combine with Perfect, the Aspect used to indicate a completed action or terminated state. The two Aspects are also used separately, of course. Perfect is found in either [+ Past] or [– Past], the distinction being one of 'relevance': [– Past] combines with Perfect when the action communicated by the verb has relevance to present time (see sentence (125)); [+ Past] is employed when the completed action had implications for a subsequent action occurring before present time (see (126) and (129)).

One obscure Aspect in English is what might be called 'Habitual'. Two variants of this Aspect were illustrated in (118), (128). They differ in that one states a quasi-permanent fact and the other an immutable truth: the situation described in (118) can change if 'I' takes on a new job, whereas the truth of (128) depends on a constant physical fact or at least the acceptance of a physical definition. This difference is reflected in the fact that the variety of Habitual Aspect utilized in (118) can be combined with [+Past], while (128) cannot be put in the past without becoming absurd:

(130)   I used to be a teacher.
(131)   (?*)Water used to boil at 100° Centigrade.

A variant of Habitual which is perhaps intermediate between the usages illustrated by (118) and (128) is represented by

(132)   London is situated on the River Thames.

Although (133) is possible, it affronts the apparent permanence of the statement, though not to the extent (131) does:

(133)   London used to be situated on the River Thames.

Finally, a further variant of Habitual, which might be called 'Iterative', is illustrated by

(134)   I go to London every Tuesday.

Contrast the simple Habitual:

(135)   I don't eat meat.

Habitual, Perfect and Progressive might be regarded as 'special' Aspects – as signalling deviations from the aspectual norm. What is the neutral aspectual state? Is there a 'simple past' or 'simple present'? Certainly, [+Past] seems to be associated with a neutral Aspect, which we might call 'Momentary':

(123)   I closed the door.
(136)   The teacher shouted at him.

These forms seem to be more 'basic' than, say, *I had closed the door*, *The teacher was shouting at him*. But there seems to be no natural mechanism in English for expressing present-time momentary action. There is, it is true, the 'demonstrative' usage, as in

(137)   I switch the cleaner on, thus. (Salesman switches it on.)

But the nearest we can come to a momentary present is, generally, in sentences displaying [−Past] tense and *Progressive* Aspect: *I'm switching the cleaner on*.

Voice, like Aspect, is not fully understood as yet. The most informative way in which I can express its function is to say that it provides contrasting ways of picking out the 'agency' of an action in Subject-Verb-Object statements. A contrast in agency in English is maintained by the Active and Passive Voices, illustrated in (138) and (139); but other emphases are achieved, as we can see from (140)–(142):

(138)　A cop shot the demonstrator.
(139)　The demonstrator was shot by a cop.
(140)　Someone shot the demonstrator.
(141)　The demonstrator was shot by someone.
(142)　The demonstrator was shot.

We might say that (138)–(142) show a decreasing emphasis on the agency of the shooting. There is not space here to comment on the 'someone' uses (see p. 97 below); but (142), in which the agent is unspecified, is of particular interest. Given just (138) and (139), one might wonder what the function of the Passive is, since the two sentences (and all similar pairs) are virtual paraphrases of each other. (142) 'justifies' the Passive. It is probably derived from an intermediate structure which is very similar to that of (139). In this intermediate structure, the agent is specified obliquely (*by* + *NP*) in order to facilitate its subsequent deletion, giving a primary contrast between (138) – agent explicitly mentioned – and (142) – agent unexpressed. For further discussion, see Ch. 8, pp. 96–8.

We turn to the fourth system under *Aux*, Mood. This very complicated, and as yet poorly understood, system expresses the speaker's attitude to, confidence in, or rhetorical orientation towards, the topic of the sentence. For instance, the auxiliary *will*, now used to indicate future time, is descended from the Anglo-Saxon verb *willan*, which meant 'have the intention to': it attested to one's commitment to an action which was to be undertaken in the future. It expressed attitude rather than simple time. Compare modern English *may* in (143), which indicates possibility or uncertainty – a reduced degree of the certainty expressed by the old *will*, and certainly not primarily a temporal meaning:

(143)　I may go to London next week.

May, will, must, need to, etc., all express 'marked' or positively specified choices under Mood. These contrast with each other and with the unmarked or neutral choice of 'Indicative' Mood, the Mood of plain statement conveying no special stance or engagement on the part of the speaker. See, for example, (144) and (145):

(144)　I'm writing a book.
(145)　The orchestra was disappointing.

or any of the sentences (123)–(129) above. Notice that none of these sentences manifests any of the special words (*can, will*, etc.)

associated with the classic 'marked' modals, or any of the rearrangements of morphemes found in Interrogatives, Imperatives, Negatives and Affirmatives, all of which I will treat, provisionally, as Moods.

'Marked' modal systems in English include the following: *Possibility/Certainty*. This is a scale of degrees of certainty communicated by the speaker; the following indicate various degrees of confidence in the truth of the statement:

(146)　He may have done it.
(147)　He must have done it.
(148)　He might do it.
(149)　He will do it.

The system underlying (146)–(149) connects with both the plain Indicative (*He has done it*) and with the *Affirmative* Mood (sometimes called 'Emphatic'), in which the speaker is especially assertive, claiming the truth of his statement against the possibility or reality of a denial:

(150)　He múst have done it.
(151)　I wíll do it.

Notice that the affirmative stress ′ is just as clearly a communicator of syntactic meaning as is a full morpheme such as *can* or *will*.

(152) represents a type of sentence which is a perennial embarrassment to children and source of anger to teachers:

(152)　Can I leave the room?

Modern English usage has established *can* as ambiguous between 'be able to' and 'be allowed to'. In the second of these two senses, *can* is a modal verb which expresses a Mood of *Permission*; it is thus synonymous with *may*, which is purely modal and has the sense 'be allowed to' in such sentences as the following:

(153)　You may leave the room.

Can in the sense of 'be able to' is probably not to be considered as a modal – I do not think we should set up a Mood 'Ability' to account for sentences such as (154):

(154)　I can do anything better than you can.

Interestingly, the Anglo-Saxon ancestor of *can* (*cunnan*) was probably not a modal verb.

Another system, which might be called *Obligation* or *Necessity*, may form a separate Mood or may, like *can* in the sense of 'be able to', be a simple lexical matter. I am inclined to the former interpretation: that the following sentences, for example, are modally 'marked':

(155) I ought to go home.
(156) I must go and visit her.
(157) I should have worn my seat belt.
(158) I need to have a tooth filled.

Finally, in the present account I will treat *Interrogative, Imperative* and *Negative* as Moods, even though this interpretation has not been fully justified. There are many unanswered questions about these three structures, but, as we will see in Ch. 8, the present interpretation at least allows us to propose quite a simple set of transformational processes. For the moment, here are some examples:

(159) Did you finish your work?
(160) What are you reading?
(161) Go away.
(162) Please eat your dinner.
(163) He didn't finish the book.
(164) He never finished a book.

We cannot help noticing the great variety of superficial structures underlain by *Aux*: single morphemes inserted before the verb (*will, n't*), deletion (Imperative), increase of stress (Affirmative), suffixes attached to the verb (*-ed, -ing*). Whatever system of underlying features is eventually, in a more definitive grammar, assigned to *Aux*, and whatever T-rules are devised, in the fashion of those given on pp. 64–7 above for *Det*, to arrange these features into alternative sets, it is obvious that the route between the finally formed set and the related morphemes of surface structure will be indirect and quite variable from case to case. This route is, of course, mapped by a sequence of *realization rules*, as mentioned on p. 67 above.

To conclude this chapter I will illustrate some of the realization rules which carry *Det* through to surface structure. An example of the realization of *Aux* will be found in the next chapter, p. 82.

The output from the sequence of T-rules which develops *Det* is a pair of feature-sets. The left-hand set is a particular selection of features of *Det*; the right-hand symbol uniquely specifies a particular noun. To the right of this there is (if the *NP* concerned is the Subject) a string of symbols which identify the Predicate-Phrase, and since these symbols do not affect the realization of *NP*, we will simply note their presence, using the cover symbol *Y*; if the *NP* is the Object, the cover symbol *Y* stands for 'nothing'; similarly, *X* stands for whatever is to the left of the *NP*.

One possible input to the realization rules is

$$X + \begin{bmatrix} +\text{Pl} \\ +\text{Def} \end{bmatrix} + boy + Y$$

(The lexical item *boy* is quoted here as a notational abbreviation for a set of syntactic/semantic features defining a specific *N*.) A highly particularized rule is applied which turns the *Det* in question into the morphemes which express it in surface structure:

(a) $X + \begin{bmatrix} +Pl \\ +Def \end{bmatrix} + N + Y \Rightarrow X + (the + \text{-}s) + N + Y$

Notice how the rule develops the article *the* and the plural inflexion *-s* simultaneously from *Det*, thus acknowledging the essential relationship which they have by virtue of their common origin in *Det*. Note also that *the* is not a simple substitute for [+Def], nor *-s* for [+Pl]: the two morphemes reflect a *complex* meaning in *Det*, not *two separate* meanings from *Det*.

Next, the output string of the particularized rule is subjected to a very much more general T-rule which determines the relative positions of elements:

(b) $X + Af + N + Y \Rightarrow X + N + Af + Y$

(where Af ≡ affix, X ≡ anything to the left of the affix – *the* in this case – and Y ≡ anything to the right of the *N*). The output of this rule is the string

the + boy + -s

which becomes the input to the phonological component of the grammar and is eventually phonetically represented as *the boys*.

Often there is, superficially, no affix: with *the boys* compare *the boy*. To meet this eventuality, we introduce the symbol Ø 'zero' in intermediate strings:

$X + \begin{bmatrix} -Pl \\ +Def \end{bmatrix} + boy + Y$

$X + (the + \text{Ø}) + boy + Y$ (by a particular rule analogous to (a))

$X + the + boy + \text{Ø} + Y$ (by rule (b))

Ø can be used twice, as in the derivation of the Subject-*NP* of *John writes*:

$X + \begin{bmatrix} -Pl \\ -Univ \end{bmatrix} + John + Y$

$X + (\text{Ø} + \text{Ø}) + John + Y$ (by a rule analogous to (a))

$X + \text{Ø} + John + \text{Ø} + Y$ (by rule (b))

More complicated *NP*s are realized by a slightly more complicated process but one which follows just the same principles:

74

$$X + \begin{bmatrix} +\text{Pl} \\ +\text{Def} \\ +\text{Cardinal} \end{bmatrix} + boy + Y$$

$X +$ *(the* + *-s)* + Cardinal + *boy* + Y   (by a rule analogous to (a))
$X +$ *the* + Cardinal + *-s* + *boy* + Y   (by a permutation rule)
$X +$ *the* + Cardinal + *boy* + *-s* + Y   (by rule (b))

Now a supplementary lexical insertion rule replaces [Cardinal] by a cardinal number other than *one*:

the + *three* + *boy* + *-s*

This is the input to the phonology and will become *the three boys* in due course.

The realization rules are a combination of very specific and very general rules. There have to be a large number of particular rules (rules like (a)), but overall the method is much more economical than cruder methods such as listing the occurring morpheme-sequences or classifying the occurring morphemes and writing rules for the orders in which they appear.

Exercises and topics for discussion

1. Provide and discuss some general definitions of *Det* and *Aux*.
2. In the face of such sentences as *John sleeps, Man is mortal, I am a teacher*, why do we assert that *Det* is obligatory? What are the implications of this assertion?
3. Some words which are apparently outside *Det* and *Aux* could be said to have deictic properties: *come, arrive, go, depart, near, far, yesterday, today, tomorrow, now, then*, etc. Extend this list of examples, referring to material from languages other than English if you can, and discuss the prospects for accommodating these facts in a grammar of the present kind.
4. Construct transformational rules for introducing the optional features [Cardinal], [Ordinal] and [Quant] into a feature-set for *Det*. (You might like to take the rule for [Prox], p. 66 above, as a model.) List plenty of illustrative sentences to indicate the range of the materials you are accounting for.
5. Give a feature representation of the underlying structure of the italicized *NP*s in the following sentences and work out how these come to be realized in surface structure:

    (a) *These boys* are a nuisance.
    (b) *Man* is mortal.
    (c) *Some people* can't be trusted.
    (d) *Some people* were running away.

(e) *The third place* went to Mr Smith.

(f) *A few people* were running away.

(g) *All men* are mortal.

6. Some features of *Aux* may be used together – e.g. Negative and Affirmative in *I didn't do it* or Negative and Interrogative as in *Why didn't you follow the instructions?*, but not Negative and Indicative, or Indicative and Affirmative. Concentrating particularly but not exclusively on Mood, discuss permissible and non-permissible combinations.

7. Provide derivations for the following sentences, beginning with *S* and proceeding as far as the techniques of Chs. 3–6 will allow you:

(a) Rover has eaten the steak.

(b) These two pupils may be brilliant.

(c) Pigs can't fly.

seven

Derivation of a Simple Sentence

In this chapter I will go through the derivation of one simple sentence in detail. The method will be to give a sequential derivation, in which each line is derived from the preceding one by the application of one rule to just one symbol. (Actually, a rule is applied to one string and changes one symbol, or feature contained in a symbol, at a time.) Rewriting rules are followed by various kinds of transformational rules: lexical insertion rules, rules for expanding *Det* and *Aux*, and realization rules. In general, the T-rules follow one another in derivations in the order just stated. In the display below, I will intersperse notes on the rules employed with the lines of the derivation. The target sentence is

(165)   Peter opened the window.

This is a 'simple' sentence in the technical sense of containing only one underlying P-marker; its tree-structure is as follows:

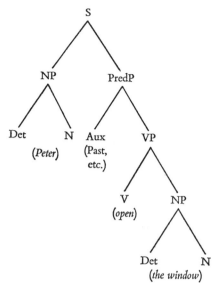

The derivation begins with the grammar's initial symbol *S*, and proceeds to line (6), a terminal string of the base, by application of a selection from the base rewriting rules:

(1) S
(2) NP + PredP   (by rule (i) of p. 35)
(3) Det + N + PredP   (by rule (iii))
(4) Det + N + Aux + VP   (by rule (ii), second line)
(5) Det + N + Aux + V + NP   (by rule (iv), first line)
(6) Det + N + Aux + V + Det + N   (by rule (iii))

Line (6) is the input to the transformational component of the syntax. The first step after the base rules have been applied is lexical interpretation of the *N* functioning as the Subject. There are no constraints on what *N* may occur here; in this instance, a cluster of syntactic/semantic features uniquely identifying the lexical item *Peter* is substituted for *N*:

(7)
$$\text{Det} + \begin{bmatrix} +\text{N} \\ +\text{Name} \\ +\text{Human} \\ +\text{Male} \\ \cdot \\ \cdot \\ \cdot \\ +\text{F}_n \end{bmatrix} + \text{Aux} + \text{V} + \text{Det} + \text{N}$$

78

(For economy of notation, the irrelevant features [. . . $+ F_n$] will be omitted henceforth wherever possible. Here I have included [+ Male] to give an example of the kind of things regarded as 'irrelevant features'. We need to know the sex of a human noun only if pronominalization occurs – *he/his, she/her* – and this does not happen in the present target sentence, so the information is not needed.)

Next, we have three lines showing the development of *Det* – development which had to await lexical interpretation of the associated *N*; these lines are formed successively by application of rules for *Det* from among those given in the previous chapter:

(8)

$$\begin{bmatrix} \text{Number} \\ \text{Universality} \end{bmatrix} + \begin{bmatrix} +\text{N} \\ +\text{Name} \\ +\text{Human} \end{bmatrix} + \text{Aux} + \text{V} + \text{Det} + \text{N}$$

(9)

$$\begin{bmatrix} -\text{Pl} \\ \text{Universality} \end{bmatrix} + \begin{bmatrix} +\text{N} \\ +\text{Name} \\ +\text{Human} \end{bmatrix} + \text{Aux} + \text{V} + \text{Det} + \text{N}$$

(10)

$$\begin{bmatrix} -\text{Pl} \\ -\text{Univ} \end{bmatrix} + \begin{bmatrix} +\text{N} \\ +\text{Name} \\ +\text{Human} \end{bmatrix} + \text{Aux} + \text{V} + \text{Det} + \text{N}$$

The Subject-*NP* is now ready for realization as a sequence of morphemes, but is held at the stage of abstract features while the remainder of the sentence is derived. The next line ((11)) shows lexical interpretation of *V*. The cluster substituted for *V* has to be selected with reference to the features present in the Subject-*NP*, remember, so it is restricted in a way that *N* was not. [+ Human], though by no means as restrictive as [− Human] or [− Animate] in the Subject would be, presumably prohibits a number of lexical items from filling the *V* position: *rain, rust, engulf* are unlikely verbs. One could also say that the feature [+ Male] bars verbs referring to biologically or typically female roles, but it is not certain that this is a grammatical matter at all. Again, the lexical insertion rule applied to this string to furnish *V* has to refer to the general characteristics of the syntax of the frame – in this case, only verbs marked [+ __NP] can be used: *open*, as here, but not *sleep*:

(11)

$$
\begin{bmatrix} -\text{Pl} \\ -\text{Univ} \end{bmatrix} + \begin{bmatrix} +\text{N} \\ +\text{Name} \\ +\text{Human} \end{bmatrix} + \text{Aux} + \begin{bmatrix} +\text{V} \\ +\_\_\text{NP} \\ +\_\_[\,-\text{Animate}] \\ +\text{Pass} \\ \cdot \\ \cdot \\ +\text{F}_n \end{bmatrix} + \text{Det} + \text{N}
$$

We now know that the right-most *NP* is an Object, since the *V* introduces a feature [+Pass] (='*Aux* may contain the feature [Passive]').

Lines (12) and (13) summarize the application of the rules for developing *Aux*, which were not stated in the previous chapter but which are quite easily formalizable in the manner adopted for *Det*:

(12)

$$
\begin{bmatrix} -\text{Pl} \\ -\text{Univ} \end{bmatrix} + \begin{bmatrix} +\text{N} \\ +\text{Name} \\ +\text{Human} \end{bmatrix} + \begin{bmatrix} \text{Tense} \\ \text{Aspect} \\ \text{Mood} \\ \text{Voice} \end{bmatrix} + \begin{bmatrix} +\text{V} \\ +\_\_\text{NP} \\ +\_\_[\,-\text{Animate}] \\ +\text{Pass} \end{bmatrix} + \text{Det} + \text{N}
$$

(13)

$$
\begin{bmatrix} -\text{Pl} \\ -\text{Univ} \end{bmatrix} + \begin{bmatrix} +\text{N} \\ +\text{Name} \\ +\text{Human} \end{bmatrix} + \begin{bmatrix} +\text{Past} \\ \text{Momentary} \\ \text{Indicative} \\ \text{Active} \end{bmatrix} + \begin{bmatrix} +\text{V} \\ +\_\_\text{NP} \\ +\_\_[\,-\text{Anim}] \end{bmatrix} + \text{Det} + \text{N}
$$

The feature [+Pass] – which means 'passivizable', not 'passive', of course – has now become irrelevant since the *Aux* cluster contains an instruction [Active] which blocks any subsequent application of the passive transformation.

Next, the *N* in the Object-*NP* is replaced by a lexical item compatible with the feature-specification for *V*:

(14)

$$
\begin{bmatrix} -\text{Pl} \\ -\text{Univ} \end{bmatrix} + \begin{bmatrix} +\text{N} \\ +\text{Name} \\ +\text{Human} \end{bmatrix} + \begin{bmatrix} +\text{Past} \\ \text{Mom} \\ \text{Ind} \\ \text{Act} \end{bmatrix} + \begin{bmatrix} +\text{V} \\ +\_\_\text{NP} \\ +\_\_[\,-\text{Anim}] \end{bmatrix} + \text{Det} + \begin{bmatrix} +\text{N} \\ +\text{Count} \\ -\text{Anim} \\ \cdot \\ \cdot \\ +\text{F}_n \end{bmatrix}
$$

The right-most *N* has now been specified as *window*, and is expressed in a feature notation which will allow us to choose a *Det* for it; this next stage requires four rules, and all are obligatory:

(15)
$$\begin{bmatrix} -\text{Pl} \\ -\text{Univ} \end{bmatrix} + \begin{bmatrix} +\text{N} \\ +\text{Name} \\ +\text{Human} \end{bmatrix} + \begin{bmatrix} +\text{Past} \\ \text{Mom} \\ \text{Ind} \\ \text{Act} \end{bmatrix} + \begin{bmatrix} +\text{V} \\ +\_\text{NP} \end{bmatrix} + \begin{bmatrix} \text{Number} \\ \text{Universality} \end{bmatrix} +$$
$$\begin{bmatrix} +\text{N} \\ +\text{Count} \end{bmatrix}$$

(16)
$$\begin{bmatrix} -\text{Pl} \\ -\text{Univ} \end{bmatrix} + \begin{bmatrix} +\text{N} \\ +\text{Name} \\ +\text{Human} \end{bmatrix} + \begin{bmatrix} +\text{Past} \\ \text{Mom} \\ \text{Ind} \\ \text{Act} \end{bmatrix} + \begin{bmatrix} +\text{V} \\ +\_\text{NP} \end{bmatrix} + \begin{bmatrix} -\text{Pl} \\ \text{Universality} \end{bmatrix} +$$
$$\begin{bmatrix} +\text{N} \\ +\text{Count} \end{bmatrix}$$

(17)
$$\begin{bmatrix} -\text{Pl} \\ -\text{Univ} \end{bmatrix} + \begin{bmatrix} +\text{N} \\ +\text{Name} \\ +\text{Human} \end{bmatrix} + \begin{bmatrix} +\text{Past} \\ \text{Mom} \\ \text{Ind} \\ \text{Act} \end{bmatrix} + \begin{bmatrix} +\text{V} \\ +\_\text{NP} \end{bmatrix} + \begin{bmatrix} -\text{Pl} \\ -\text{Univ} \end{bmatrix} +$$
$$\begin{bmatrix} +\text{N} \\ +\text{Count} \end{bmatrix}$$

(18)
$$\begin{bmatrix} -\text{Pl} \\ -\text{Univ} \end{bmatrix} + \begin{bmatrix} +\text{N} \\ +\text{Name} \\ +\text{Human} \end{bmatrix} + \begin{bmatrix} +\text{Past} \\ \text{Mom} \\ \text{Ind} \\ \text{Act} \end{bmatrix} + \begin{bmatrix} +\text{V} \\ +\_\text{NP} \end{bmatrix} + \begin{bmatrix} -\text{Pl} \\ +\text{Def} \end{bmatrix} +$$
$$\begin{bmatrix} +\text{N} \\ +\text{Count} \end{bmatrix}$$

Accepting the convention that the exponents of lexical symbols are given in shorthand here, we now have a detailed symbolization of a unique sentence in terms of syntactic and semantic features. We have assigned an explicit structural description to it, and nothing more can be said about its meaning. The final stages of the derivation are quite mechanical: we now proceed to utilize realization rules to turn line (18) into a sequence of morphemes. Like the T-rules which have been used up to this point, the realization rules are progressive, working in cycles to replace feature-sets by morphemes left-to-right along the string. Notice that each realization typically involves two stages: first, insertion of morphemes, by a specific rule (cf. rule (a), p. 74 above), and then positioning of them according to some more general rule such as (b). At this point I will replace the feature-symbolization of the lexical items by the 'real words' *Peter, open* and *window* – this is only a notational change, for these very specific meanings have already been present in the derivation, in abbreviated feature-symbolization, from lines (7), (11) and (14). The first two applications of realization rules refer to the Subject-*NP*:

(19)
$$(\emptyset \ldots \emptyset) + Peter + \begin{bmatrix} +\text{Past} \\ \text{Mom} \\ \text{Ind} \\ \text{Act} \end{bmatrix} + open + \begin{bmatrix} -\text{Pl} \\ +\text{Def} \end{bmatrix} + window$$

(20)
$$\emptyset + Peter + \emptyset + \begin{bmatrix} +\text{Past} \\ \text{Mom} \\ \text{Ind} \\ \text{Act} \end{bmatrix} + open + \begin{bmatrix} -\text{Pl} \\ +\text{Def} \end{bmatrix} + window$$

Now we turn to *Aux*. This particular realization has not yet been illustrated. In effect, all the components of *Aux* have to be scrutinized and those which have no expression in surface structure discarded; in this case, all except [+Past] disappear:

(21) $\emptyset + \text{Peter} + \emptyset + [\,+\text{Past}] + open + \begin{bmatrix} -\text{Pl} \\ +\text{Def} \end{bmatrix} + window$

Now [+Past] is replaced by the morpheme sequence $(\emptyset \ldots -ed)$:

(22) $\emptyset + Peter + \emptyset + (\emptyset + -ed) + open + \begin{bmatrix} -\text{Pl} \\ +\text{Def} \end{bmatrix} + window$

($\emptyset$ is inserted in the replacement for [+Past] to preserve symmetry with the several other two-morpheme realizations of *Aux*: cf. *has opened* (*have . . .-ed*) and *is opening* (*be . . . -ing*). Illustrations of more complex realizations of *Aux* will be found in the next chapter.) As the next step in the present derivation, we apply a repositioning rule exactly analogous to the one for *Det* which was given on p. 74 above and which is used in the present derivation between lines (19) and (20) and (24) and (25). The rule in this case is

$$X + Af + V + Y \Rightarrow X + V + Af + Y$$

and it yields the line

(23) $\emptyset + Peter + \emptyset + \emptyset + open + -ed + \begin{bmatrix} -\text{Pl} \\ +\text{Def} \end{bmatrix} + window$

Our last two steps realize the Object-*NP*:

(24) $\emptyset + Peter + \emptyset + \emptyset + open + -ed + (the + \emptyset) + window$
(25) $\emptyset + Peter + \emptyset + \emptyset + open + -ed + the + window + \emptyset$

Line (25) is the input to the phonological component of the grammar. At this next stage, the italicized words and morphemes are given the phonemic 'spellings' which are stored for them in the dictionary from which the lexical items were drawn in the form of syntactic and semantic features. Phonological rules apply to these phonemic spellings: for instance, the morpheme *-ed* – which in lines (22)–(25) above was not meant to indicate a pronunciation, but only an abstract syntactic formative – is phonetically represented as the voiced alveolar stop /d/ in relation to *open*, whereas it would be /t/ if affixed to *work* and /id/ or /əd/ if *V* were *want*. Phonological rules also insert word-boundaries, and their associated phonetic transitions, in appropriate places, and finally the whole sentence is endowed with a suitable stress-and-pitch contour. It is now 'pronounceable': that is to say, we have now explained the way it sounds as well as the way it means.

This sample derivation has been intended to gather all the processes so far covered into one place, and illustrate the mechanics of their operation and interaction. Of course, not everything can be illustrated in one derivation, since one has to choose a particular sentence and therefore some types of structure are excluded. But at least we have referred to all the *kinds* of structural operation which characterize the derivation of simple sentences: rewriting rules, lexical interpretation, the development of 'deictic' features, and realization of features as morphemes, thus finally producing a surface structure. One of the most striking aspects of linguistic description, which only a full derivation like the above can suggest really powerfully, is the way the operations concerned fit together in a very precisely ordered sequence, a chain of events between most of whose links the connection is inevitable: having taken one step, you are forced to move on to the next. As we shall see more and more in the later chapters of this book, when some of the more intricate transformations are examined, order of application of transformations is crucial: if the machine goes out of phase, it breaks down and fails to assign Structural Descriptions to sentences.

A final word on the nature of derivation, repeating a caution delivered before. A derivation is a systematic way of assigning structural descriptions to sentences and thereby making explicit the structural characteristics which speakers' linguistic competence assigns to properly-formed sentences of their language. It is not a model for the *production* of sentences, nor, if read backwards, is it a model of how listeners *understand* sentences. Careful examination of our derivation will suggest that it becomes preposterous if we suggest that it reflects sequential 'inner behaviour' on the part of the speaker before he utters each of his sentences.

Exercises and topics for discussion

1. Write derivations for the following sentences:

    (a) Dogs bark.
    (b) That sunset is beautiful.

2. Explore some of the reasons why a derivation is not a plausible model of linguistic production; define the concept of 'derivation'.
3. What is the status of the italicized words and morphemes in the following sentences? Explain, informally, in each case, their origins in deep structure.

    (a) *Did* you like the play?
    (b) Nicholas *has been* visit*ing* Scotland.
    (c) This sentence *isn't* very clear.
    (d) *Many* hands make *light* work.
    (e) *All of these* men are guilty.
    (f) John *was* disown*ed* by his father.

4. It is said that rewriting rules do not make reference to existing structure, while transformational rules do. Investigate this notion of 'making reference to existing structure'.

eight

Negatives, Passives, Questions and Similar Structures

In the interests of providing a simple example for the sample derivation, I chose in (165) a collection of features of *Aux* which entailed as little as possible complexity in surface structure and hence an uncomplicated sequence of realization rules. In this chapter I will describe some more complex arrangements for which various configurations of features from *Aux* are responsible, and in particular some distinctive constructions which have especially interested transformationalists from the earliest days of this modern approach to syntax.

But first, we look at one other characteristic of surface structure which (165) happened not to illustrate: *agreement* (sometimes called *concord*). This is a situation in which some syntactic information is given more than once in the surface realization of a sentence. The most familiar examples, for most readers, will probably be drawn from highly inflected languages like French and Latin where adjectives agree with nouns and verbs agree with nouns. A French noun belongs to one or other of two genders: masculine or feminine. (This distinction has almost nothing to do with the sex-distinction, and applies to inanimate as well as animate nouns.) The gender of a noun is reflected in the article which accompanies it (*le* or *la*, *un* or *une*) and in the ending of any adjective which relates to it:

(166) un arbre vert
(167) une maison verte

Similarly, the ending of the adjective reflects Number in the *NP*:

(166)   un arbre vert
(168)   les arbres verts

Latin enjoyed a similar system, as did Anglo-Saxon, but this inflexional redundancy has disappeared in modern English. Again, French and Latin verbs respond to the Number of the *NP* and, where the *NP* is a pronoun, to the Person of the pronoun:

(169)   domin*us* servos am*at*   [– Pl] [III Pers]
(170)   domin*i* servos am*ant*   [+ Pl] [III Pers]
(171)   patriam am*o*   [– Pl] [I Pers]

The remnants of an agreement system are evident in the English verb. It affects all verbs when they are [– Past], and the auxiliary *be* in [+ Past] too. [– Past] verbs have the affix *-s* when the Subject-*NP* contains [– Pl], and Ø when the Subject is [+ Pl]; *be* employs quite distinct words for singular and plural:

(172)   Peter opens the window.
(173)   Doormen open doors.
(174)   This apple is sweet.
(175)   These apples are sour.

No variation is found as between [+ Pl] and [– Pl] when the verb is [+ Past], except where the auxiliary *be* is concerned:

(176)   Peter/the children enjoyed the film.
(177)   The apple was sweet.
(178)   The apples were sour.

Finally, there are more complicated patterns when the Subject is a pronoun; verbs are sensitive to the 'person' of pronouns:

I
you
we   } sleep
they

he
she   } sleeps
it

I   am
you }
we   } are
they }   } tired
he   }
she } is
it   }

I   }
he   } was
she   }
it   }   } tired
you   }
we   } were
they   }

But there are simpler patterns with most of the 'modal auxiliaries': *will, may, shall, can* ([+ Past] *would, might, should, could*) are invariable in relation to number and person.

These facts are well known. What we have to consider is how to represent them in a transformational grammar. One thing is clear: that there is redundancy in surface structure – compare *a dog barks*, where *dog*Ø signals [– Pl] just as much as *barks*, and *dogs bark*, where *bark*Ø only duplicates the information [+ Pl] given by *dogs*. Now number is basic to the *NP* (it is a feature of *Det*) and not intrinsic to *V* or *Aux*. Similarly, in French and Latin gender is inherent in *N*, and is reflected in *Adj* merely for convenience or by accident. (Inflecting Latin adjectives for gender and number is functional because it associates an adjective and the noun it modifies, an association not evident in the unpredictable word-order: it serves no function in French because which adjectives go with which nouns can be inferred from word-order.) The redundancy introduced by agreement suggests that we should represent number (and person and gender where applicable) only *once* in underlying structure, in the basic position – within *Det* for number and person, in the feature-set for *N* for gender. A local transformation can later be applied to repeat the information in secondary, derived, positions. A satisfactory rule for English would be

$$[\text{Number}] + N + Aux + X \Rightarrow [\text{Number}] + N + Aux + [\text{Number}] + X$$

So a string of the form (a) would become (b) under the above transformation:

(a)
$$\begin{bmatrix} -\text{Pl} \\ -\text{Univ} \end{bmatrix} + \begin{bmatrix} +\text{N} \\ +\text{Name} \end{bmatrix} + \begin{bmatrix} -\text{Past} \\ \text{Mom} \\ \text{Ind} \\ \text{Act} \end{bmatrix} + \begin{bmatrix} +\text{V} \\ +\text{Pass} \end{bmatrix} + \begin{bmatrix} -\text{Pl} \\ +\text{Def} \end{bmatrix} + \begin{bmatrix} +\text{N} \\ +\text{Count} \end{bmatrix}$$

(b)
$$\begin{bmatrix} -\text{Pl} \\ -\text{Univ} \end{bmatrix} + \begin{bmatrix} +\text{N} \\ +\text{Name} \end{bmatrix} + \begin{bmatrix} -\text{Past} \\ \text{Mom} \\ \text{Ind} \\ \text{Act} \end{bmatrix} + [-\text{Pl}] + \begin{bmatrix} +\text{V} \\ +\text{Pass} \end{bmatrix} + \begin{bmatrix} -\text{Pl} \\ +\text{Def} \end{bmatrix} + \begin{bmatrix} +\text{N} \\ +\text{Count} \end{bmatrix}$$

Later, the third and fourth segments will be amalgamated as $\begin{bmatrix} -\text{Past} \\ -\text{Pl} \end{bmatrix}$ which is the 'affix' to be repositioned after *V*, where it becomes the source of the morpheme *-s* rather than Ø: *Peter opens the window*.

This rule for introducing morphological redundancy must be applied at a certain appropriate point in the cycle of T-rules. The importance of a set order is proved by passive constructions, in which the verb agrees with the superficial Subject, not the underlying Subject:

(179)   The windows were opened by Peter.

The agreement transformation must be applied *after* the passive transformation, to prevent generation of

(180)   *The windows was opened by Peter.

in which a false agreement between *was* and *Peter* has emerged. (180) is generated if agreement takes place while the underlying Subject *Peter* is still to the left of *Aux*.

Let us now see what happens when auxiliaries more complicated than that of (165) are selected. The next simplest situation is represented by insertion of a 'modal auxiliary'; e.g.

(181)   I will go.

The *PredP* of this sentence can be partially represented as

$$\begin{bmatrix} -\text{Past} \\ \text{Intention} \end{bmatrix} + V$$

The mood [Intention] is then manifested as *will*:

$$[-\text{Past}] + will + V$$

The agreement transformation has no effect on this string and so may be ignored here; in a proper derivation, however, it has to be applied, unless the agreement rule is to be made excessively complicated by a statement of the conditions in which it does not apply. It is much easier to 'undo' the effect of the transformation at the stage of realization rules, since these rules have to be stated in terms of particular cases anyway.

Next, the affix-shifting transformation (p. 82) produces the line

$$will + [-\text{Past}] + V$$

which is realized as *will go*. If tense were [+Past], the output would be *would go*.

Note that these processes require some modifications to the affix-shifting rule: it must (a) be allowed to apply to 'auxiliary verbs' (*will, have,* etc.) as well as 'main verbs', (b) be prevented from applying twice to the same affix, otherwise undesirable strings such as *will + V + [Past] (e.g. *will walked) would be generated.

Suppose that we had an *Aux* containing [+Past, Progressive, Indicative, Active], as in

(182)   He was eating his breakfast.

[Indicative] and [Active] have no effect on the surface structure, so are ignored. The relevant representation of the part of the sentence in which we are interested is, then,

$$\begin{bmatrix} +\text{Past} \\ \text{Prog} \end{bmatrix} + V$$

which becomes $[+\text{Past}] + \textit{-ing} + V$; after repositioning of the affix this is $[+\text{Past}] + V + \textit{-ing}$. Now agreement will have operated, so in fact we have

$$\begin{bmatrix} +\text{Past} \\ -\text{Pl} \\ \text{III Pers} \end{bmatrix} + V + \textit{-ing}$$

The information within square brackets is unaffixable since *-ing* occupies the suffix position on *V*, so a supporting *be* must be introduced, giving *was* eventually. In fact, since *be* rather than *have* or *do* must be used in Progressive Aspect, *be* might be inserted at the same time as *-ing*.

A similar sequence of lines lies behind *He has eaten his breakfast* ([– Past, Perfect, Indicative, Active]), except that *-en* is the affix and *have* the tense-bearing auxiliary.

[Progressive] and [Perfect] Aspects may be selected simultaneously, as in

(183)   He had been eating his breakfast.

where *Aux* is [+ Past, (Perfect, Progressive), Indicative, Active]. The following steps are to be taken; the derivation is longer, but works on the same principles as the others; as a start, [Prog] is taken out of the *Aux* feature-set and replaced by its associated morphemes:

$$\begin{bmatrix} +\text{Past} \\ \text{Perfect} \end{bmatrix} + be + \textit{-ing} + V$$

Affix-shift reverses the third and fourth segments:

$$\begin{bmatrix} +\text{Past} \\ \text{Perfect} \end{bmatrix} + be + V + \textit{-ing}$$

Next, [Perfect] is separated from *Aux* and replaced by *have* + *-en* to the right of *Aux*:

$$[+\text{Past}] + have + \textit{-en} + be + V + \textit{-ing}$$

Affix-shift applies once again, to give

$$[+\text{Past}] + have + be + \textit{-en} + V + \textit{-ing}$$

Again we have a string to which the affix-shifting rule can be applied, and so it is:

$$have + [+Past] + be + \text{-}en + V + \text{-}ing$$

Because of the restriction that the affix-shifting transformation must not apply to the same affix twice, further applications are prevented. The above string can now be realized as *had been eating*.

A longer sequence still, such as *would have been eating*, is derived in exactly the same way, except that, in this case, insertion of the modal *will* next to [+Past] renders unnecessary the affixation of [+Past] to *have*: *will* can carry the tense marker. (Notice that in these complex superficial structures expressing *Aux* it is always the left-most element which carries tense.)

Negatives, Interrogatives, Imperatives and Affirmatives, and the Passive Voice, all entail similar derivational processes. Several rather different ways of accounting for these constructions have been proposed; what is clear in all proposals is that these constructions must have distinctive origins in deep structure, and not result merely from different kinds of transformational processing after underlying structure has been established. The strategy adopted in this account is to derive each of the first four from an appropriate modal feature available under *Aux* in the base syntax, and Passive similarly from the Voice dimension of *Aux*. So the presence of a feature, say [Neg], in the specification for *Aux* would set in action a sequence of realization rules to give a surface structure for, say, a negative rather than indicative construction:

$$NP + \begin{bmatrix} +Past \\ Mom \\ Neg \\ Act \end{bmatrix} + V + NP$$

$$NP + [+Past] + [Neg] + V + NP$$

([Neg] is *not* an affix, so the affix-shifting transformation is not applied.)

$$NP + [+Past] + do + [Neg] + V + NP$$

Do is inserted to carry [+Past], since [Neg] separates it from *V*; next, [+Past] and *do* are transposed:

$$NP + do + [+Past] + [Neg] + V + NP$$
$$NP + did + [Neg] + V + NP$$
$$NP + did + n't + V + NP$$

(e.g. (184) Peter didn't open the window).

Simple yes/no questions are realized by a change of word-order, rather than, as with negatives, by insertion of a special morpheme. The basic string is

$$NP + \begin{bmatrix} +Past \\ Mom \\ Int\ (Q) \\ Act \end{bmatrix} + V + NP$$

[Mom] and [Act] have no effect, so are discarded. [Int (Q)] causes what remains of *Aux* – in this case, [+ Past] only – to transpose with the left-most *NP*, and disappears itself:

$$[+ Past] + NP + V + NP$$

Again, *do* is introduced to provide a stem for the now unaffixable tense element, and the structure is realized as, for instance,

(185)   Did Peter open the window?

But where a modal (*can, will,* etc.) is involved, this morpheme is transferred to the beginning of the sentence with the tense element, so it is unnecessary to supply *do* to carry tense; the same is true with interrogatives combining with Perfect or Progressive Aspect: *have* or *be* moved to the beginning of the string performs this function:

(186)   Will Peter open the window?
(187)   Has John arrived?

The construction just discussed is not, of course, the only kind of question, nor is it the only way of managing yes/no questions: a rising intonation and no change in word-order may be employed:

(188)   You haven't been here before?

Here are some other types of question which must be explained in a complete grammar:

(189)   Who has opened the door?
(190)   How are cakes made?
(191)   Why should he get all the credit?
(192)   Who did the doctor visit?
(193)   Which play did they put on?
(194)   Which boy opened the door?

The difference between these and yes/no questions is that assent or denial is not demanded in relation to the whole proposition, but a query is focused on a specific part of the sentence's content, localized in a particular syntactic constituent. (190) and (191) direct the audience's attention to what in traditional grammar would be called an adverbial function: answers would begin, typically, with phrases which signal an adverbial embedded sentence in surface structure – 'by mixing flour, eggs . . .', 'because he was responsible for . . .'. (189) and (192)–(194) all query *NP*s, as do sentences of the type

(195) Where are you going? (to the cinema)
(196) When did you leave? (this morning)

I will examine here only constructions of the kinds represented in (189), (192)–(194); they belong (as do (195), (196)) to a class of questions called *WH-questions*. Since they are quite clearly distinct from yes/no questions, we must provide a different deep structure symbol, and thus a different instruction to the transformational component. Let us assume a general modal choice [Int] under *Aux*, and a subsequent obligatory choice between [Q] for yes/no questions and [WH] for WH-questions. Another line in a derivation is needed. Our [Int (Q)] of the derivation for (185) is first [Int] and then [Q], and in the following derivations [WH] presupposes a prior line containing [Int].

Our four sentences (189), (192)–(194) differ on two dimensions. (189) and (194) query an *NP* in Subject position, while (192) and (193) direct our attention to the Object. And (193) and (194) query some particular *N*, whereas (189) and (192) do not specify the *N* in respect of which the question is asked. Let us begin with (194), in which the queried *NP* is lexically specified with *boy*, and is the Subject of the underlying P-marker. At one level of representation, the deep structure is roughly as follows (I show relevant features only – *N* is fully specified, even though abbreviated here):

$$\begin{bmatrix} -\text{Pl} \\ -\text{Def} \end{bmatrix} + \begin{bmatrix} +\text{N} \\ +\text{Human} \end{bmatrix} + \begin{bmatrix} +\text{Past} \\ \text{WH} \end{bmatrix} + \text{V} + \text{NP}$$

Suppose that a transformation transfers [WH] from *Aux* to the *Det* of the *NP* immediately to its left, resulting in a string

$$\begin{bmatrix} -\text{Pl} \\ -\text{Def} \\ \text{WH} \end{bmatrix} + \begin{bmatrix} +\text{N} \\ +\text{Human} \end{bmatrix} + [+\text{Past}] + \text{V} + \text{NP}$$

Then, if the left-most symbol is a representation of *which*, we can eventually realize (194).

The alternative (189) has the *N* of the Subject-*NP* not interpreted lexically. This is not an anomalous situation, and we do not need to set up an elaborate transformational apparatus for inserting an *N* and then deleting it. As we shall see in the next chapter, many sentences containing pronouns (e.g. *He opened the door*) are similarly lexically uninterpreted at this point. For (189) we can propose an underlying representation

$$\begin{bmatrix} -\text{Pl} \\ -\text{Def} \\ \text{III} \end{bmatrix} + \begin{bmatrix} +\text{N} \\ +\text{Pron} \\ +\text{Human} \end{bmatrix} + \begin{bmatrix} -\text{Past} \\ \text{Perfect} \\ \text{WH} \end{bmatrix} + \text{V} + \text{NP}$$

[WH] is transferred to the appropriate *Det*, as above, and the resulting pair of symbols in the Subject-*NP* is amalgamated to form the basis for *who*. If the *N* in question had contained the feature [– Human], the realization would have been *what*.

(If the underlying representation for (189) given above had contained [Ind] instead of [Int/WH] as the modal choice under *Aux*, the following sentence would have been implied:

(197)   Someone opened the door.

Who and *someone* are both indefinite pronouns, the former interrogative.)

The above explanation of the difference between (189) and (194) can obviously be generalized to cover the difference between (192) and (193). We now enquire into what distinguishes (193) from (194) – and, by implication, (192) from (189). The underlying representation of (193) – once more simplified – must be

$$\text{NP} + \begin{bmatrix} +\text{Past} \\ \text{WH} \end{bmatrix} + \text{V} + \begin{bmatrix} -\text{Pl} \\ -\text{Def} \end{bmatrix} + \begin{bmatrix} +\text{N} \\ -\text{Human} \end{bmatrix}$$

where *NP* on the left abbreviates a pair of feature-sets underlying *they*, and the right-most feature-set is the dictionary entry for *play*. Notice that this is the same as the representation for *Did they put on a play?* except that *Aux* contains [WH] instead of [Q]. This similarity is significant, since the effect of the yes/no transformation – transposing Subject-*NP* and *Aux* – is needed in this type of WH-question also; *Aux* is shifted to the beginning of the string:

$$\begin{bmatrix} +\text{Past} \\ \text{WH} \end{bmatrix} + \text{NP} + \text{V} + \begin{bmatrix} -\text{Pl} \\ -\text{Def} \end{bmatrix} + \begin{bmatrix} +\text{N} \\ -\text{Human} \end{bmatrix}$$

The next stage entails moving the Object-*NP* to the beginning of the sentence:

$$\begin{bmatrix} -\text{Pl} \\ -\text{Def} \end{bmatrix} + \begin{bmatrix} +\text{N} \\ -\text{Human} \end{bmatrix} + \begin{bmatrix} +\text{Past} \\ \text{WH} \end{bmatrix} + \text{NP} + \text{V}$$

Now the next step is identical to one taken in the course of deriving (189): moving the interrogative feature [WH] from *Aux* to the left-most *NP*:

93

$$\begin{bmatrix} -\text{Pl} \\ -\text{Def} \\ \text{WH} \end{bmatrix} + \begin{bmatrix} +\text{N} \\ -\text{Human} \end{bmatrix} + [\,+\text{Past}\,] + \text{NP} + \text{V}$$

At this point a surface structure can be provided, using realization rules which have already been devised to account for other constructions, representing the *Det* of the queried *NP* as *which*, and expressing [+Past] as *did*.

The constructions whose realizations have so far been demonstrated have necessitated a considerable range of types of transformational process. For a start, we have seen various permutations and transposings of formatives in the interrogative transformations as well as, on a smaller scale, in ordering the inflexional morphology of *Aux* + *V* sequences. Interrogatives also show transfer of individual features from one cluster to another. Negatives illustrate the removal of one feature from a cluster and its subsequent positioning at a particular point in a string to provide the basis for an additional morpheme (*n't*) in surface structure – a manœuvre also characteristic of the realization of Moods by way of special auxiliaries (*will, can,* etc.), and of aspectual formatives (*-en, -ing*). Agreement shows yet another process, the duplication of a feature of one cluster in another set elsewhere in the string. Such processes may interconnect in various ways, and we have had plenty of evidence of the use of several of these operations in a closely controlled sequence of transformational events. In English, perhaps the prime example of this ordered interdependency of various formally different kinds of transformation is provided by the Passive. In appearance, English Passives are the most complicated type of simple sentence (sentence based on only one underlying phrase-marker). In the light of analyses of other phenomena offered in this chapter, however, there is nothing particularly remarkable about the derivation of Passives: all the procedures which are needed have already been illustrated.

In surface structure, Passives differ from corresponding Actives in three ways:

(198)   A cop shot the demonstrator.
(199)   The demonstrator was shot by a cop.

(= (138) and (139) of Ch. 6)

    (a) The positions of Subject- and Object-*NP*s have been transposed.
    (b) *By* has been introduced before the relocated Subject-*NP*.

(c) A special verb morphology – classically *be* + -*en* as in *was eaten*, but obscured in the irregular verb *shoot* – is used; contrast *be* + -*ing* for Progressive Aspect, *have* + -*en* for Perfect.

These are not unfamiliar processes; all we need to do here is discover their order of application in the metaphorical 'time-scheme' of a derivation. The first significant choice occurs in the lexical interpretation of V: if the lexical feature-set substituted for V contains [+Pass], then, when selection of features for *Aux* takes place, the feature [Pass] may be chosen. As we saw in Ch. 5, this condition is a precaution against the generation of ungrammatical sentences like (75) *Three tons are weighed by this truck*. This condition is met by the verb *shoot*, so we can go ahead and include [Pass] in *Aux*; here is the notation for, e.g. (199) (as usual, simplified – it is assumed that the two *N*s and the *V* are fully specified):

$$NP + \begin{bmatrix} +Past \\ Mom \\ Ind \\ Pass \end{bmatrix} + V + NP$$

[Mom] and [Ind] have no effect on the realization, so are dropped; and at the next stage [+Past] and [Pass] are separated:

$$NP_1 + [+Past] + [Pass] + V + NP_2$$

As a notational convenience, I have numbered the two *NP*s – this would not be necessary in a fully written-out derivation, since they would be distinguished by their feature specifications. The first effect of the presence of [Pass] is to reverse these *NP*s:

$$NP_2 + [+Past] + [Pass] + V + NP_1$$

Notice that [Pass] is retained, for it has more work to do; next, it causes *by* to be inserted before the repositioned NP_1:

$$NP + [+Past] + [Pass] + V + by + NP$$

Now it is replaced by a sequence of formatives *be* + -*en*:

$$NP + [+Past] + be + \text{-}en + V + by + NP$$

Now that the feature [Pass] has completed its sequence of operations, the agreement transformation can be applied. This has the effect of repeating the [–Pl] of the left-most *NP* in the now reduced representation of *Aux*:

$$NP + \begin{bmatrix} +Past \\ -Pl \end{bmatrix} + be + \text{-}en + V + by + NP$$

Next, the affix-shifting rule applies twice in succession:

$$NP + \begin{bmatrix} +\text{Past} \\ -\text{Pl} \end{bmatrix} + be + V + \text{-}en + by + NP$$

$$NP + be + \begin{bmatrix} +\text{Past} \\ -\text{Pl} \end{bmatrix} + V + \text{-}en + by + NP$$

This string of symbols may now be rendered as a sequence of morphemes. $Be + \begin{bmatrix} +\text{Past} \\ -\text{Pl} \end{bmatrix}$ becomes *was*; *-en* is realized as Ø because

the verb *shoot* inhibits the affix *-en*, but the vowel /u/ of *shoot* changes to /ɒ/: *shot*. (Contrast *eaten*, which employs *-en*, and *lifted*, in which *-en* underlies the surface morpheme *-ed*.) Finally, the syntactic processing gives way to phonological interpretation.

At this point in the argument, a general comment on the relationship between Actives and Passives may be made. It would be very easy to regard (199) *The demonstrator was shot by a cop* as a 'derived version' of (198) *A cop shot the demonstrator*. One might say that (199) is simply a more involved way of saying exactly the same as (198), and that (198) is evidently a more 'basic' form of statement. If that is tantamount to saying that (199) is *derived from* (198), then the formulation is exceedingly misleading. It is *not* the function of transformational rules *to derive one sentence* – simpler as with imperatives, more complicated as with passives – *from another sentence* which is in some way 'basic'. Transformations do happen to relate sentences to one another, but not in that way; not in the way that this erroneous diagram would suggest:

$$S \xrightarrow[\text{PSG rules}]{} \text{Active} \xrightarrow[\text{T-rules}]{} \text{Passive.}$$

T-rules in fact relate sentences by defining partially overlapping derivations, thus:

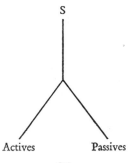

The common path shows a shared derivation up to a certain stage; for (198) and (199) the shared path extends a long way, because they have all their lexical items in common. The point where the paths fork is the derivational stage at which [Act] or [Pass] is chosen in *Aux*. (198) and (199) are parallel structures, and derivations show what they share and in what respects they differ.

On p. 71 above I compared three other sentences with (198) and (199), asking the question: what is the justification for the Passive? I repeat all five sentences here:

(198)   A cop shot the demonstrator.
(199)   The demonstrator was shot by a cop.
(200)   Someone shot the demonstrator.
(201)   The demonstrator was shot by someone.
(202)   The demonstrator was shot.

It was suggested that (202) is the real justification for the Passive: the situation in which the agent is left totally unarticulated, so that the emphasis is all on the action and its object and not on the instigator of that action. It is obvious that (202) is not derived from the underlying structure of (198) and (199); but (200) and (201) show how it arises. *Someone* is an indefinite pronoun; it is also an *NP*, and it has the underlying representation

$$\begin{bmatrix} -Pl \\ -Def \end{bmatrix} + \begin{bmatrix} +N \\ +Pron \\ +Human \end{bmatrix}$$

Since it is a properly formed *NP*, then, given a verb marked [+Pass] (and, by implication, as all verbs are, [+Act]), either (200) or (201) can be generated according to the conventions already illustrated. (202) can be accounted for by an extra transformation. If there is a string

$$\begin{bmatrix} -Pl \\ -Def \end{bmatrix} + \begin{bmatrix} +N \\ +Pron \\ +Human \end{bmatrix} + Aux + \begin{bmatrix} +V \\ +Pass \end{bmatrix} + NP$$

and if [Pass] is chosen in *Aux*, then a string which might underlie (201) can be formed in the normal way. Optionally, we can go a stage further: given the string

$$NP + [+Past] + be + \text{-}en + V + by + \begin{bmatrix} -Pl \\ -Def \end{bmatrix} + \begin{bmatrix} +N \\ +Pron \\ +Human \end{bmatrix}$$

we can delete the last three segments in the string, to give a string which might underlie (202). By this derivational sequence, we show

97

(a) that (202) is a passive construction – one of its derivation lines is the underlying string for a regular Passive like (201) – despite appearances; and (b) that (202) is not specially related to any particular surface structure such as (199). The arrangement of this derivation thus reveals two very important facts which speakers of English know about sentences (198)–(202).

In deriving (202), no fully specified lexical item was deleted; the same is true of deletion in the derivation of Imperatives. Readers' analysis of Imperatives is invited in an exercise below; the general conventions established in this chapter should be an adequate guide to the solution of the problem.

Exercises and topics for discussion

1. Discuss the importance of the order of application of transformational rules.
2. Give your own examples of the following processes:

   (a) permutation transformations.
   (b) agreement transformations handling *gender*.
   (c) deletion transformations.

3. Show how the verbal phrases (including *Aux*) of the following sentences pass from the stage of abstract representation by features to the stage of concrete representation by morphemes:

   (a) John must be joking.
   (b) I was being flippant.
   (c) Would you have taken that decision?
   (d) I díd close the door.
   (e) Didn't you know the author?

4. Describe informally the differences between the predicates of the following sentences:

   (a) The book was interesting.
   (b) I was horrified.
   (c) She was cheated.
   (d) The plane was falling.
   (e) This book has been defaced.
   (f) I have been ill.

5. Using the analytic conventions of Ch. 8, explore the derivational history of Imperative sentences. Pay particular attention to the restrictions on the application of the imperative transformation.

6. Provide derivations for the realization stages of the following Passives:

    (a) John was failed by the examiners.
    (b) It was destroyed by a bomb.
    (c) The book was mislaid.

7. Consider how our rules for negation might be supplemented, given the following sentences:

    (a) I saw someone at the window.
    (b) I didn't see anyone at the window.
    (c) She would like some help.
    (d) She doesn't want any help.
    (e) I saw no one at the window.
    (f) No one saw me.
    (g) *Anyone didn't see me.
    (h) Someone didn't see me.
    (i) *No one didn't see me.
    (j) No, I'm not joking.

nine

Pro-forms

Many English sentences contain words which 'stand for' other words or phrases:

(203)   John defended *himself*.

Obviously, *himself* is another way of saying *John*, and the implication is that this is the same John as the John of the Subject. This substitute-word (called a *reflexive pronoun*) is an example of one type of *pro-form*; there are several other types, as can be seen from the italicized words and phrases in the following sentences:

(204)   John goes to the cinema, but Susan never goes *there*.
(205)   *I* go to the library on Saturday mornings, but *no one else* goes *there then*.
(206)   John passed the exam and *so did* Susan.
(207)   John passed the exam and Susan *did, too*.
(208)   John passed the exam and Susan failed *it*.
(209)   Peter said that *he* could never pass the exam.
(210)   *I* am not very well off.
(211)   This house will suit *us*.
(212)   John brushed *his* teeth.
(213)   *Anyone* can drive a car.
(214)   Jack fell down and then Jill *did the same*.
(215)   *I* was ill and *so* was *my* wife.

These examples show that pro-forms exist for *NP*s, verbs, adjectives and adverbs, so that, in effect, any semantic information associated with any part of constituent structure may be given in 'shorthand' form if it is repeated a second or a third time in a sentence. Now this field of pro-forms has not yet been thoroughly investigated. In particular, there are two aspects about which we would like to know more: first, the device of 'pro-formation' depends for its proper working on the fact that two meaning-bearing elements in a sentence are *co-referential*: that they denote the same object, person, process, or whatever, outside of language. For instance, in (203), before we can supply the reflexive pronoun *himself* we must know that the *John* of the Object is the same as the *John* of the Subject. That is to say, there are two distinct deep structures

(203)(a)   John defended John.
(216)   John defended John.

in the first of which *John = John* and in the second *John ≠ John*, as in

(216)(a)   John (Smith) defended John (Brown).

At the present time, TG has no formal way of showing the distinction between (203)(a) and (216) and hence no way of stating exactly the conditions under which reflexivization must occur – (203)(a) – or must not occur – (216). For the present, we will assume that this distinction can be made, although we do not yet know how to make it. Second, of the whole range of pro-forms, only the type called *pronouns* has been fully studied, and of these, only *definite* and *personal* pronouns: *I, he, they*, etc., but not *one, anyone, nobody, people*, etc.

In this chapter I will therefore concentrate on personal pronouns, including reflexive pronouns. We will investigate how they are to be represented, how they are introduced into sentences, and what restrictions apply to their use.

Sentence (209) provides a useful starting-point:

(209)   Peter said that he could never pass the exam.

This is ambiguous as between two possible references of *he*. On one interpretation, *he* has the same extra-linguistic reference as *Peter*; on the other hand, *he* may refer to a different person from Peter. These two meanings must be distinguished by different underlying representations; informally:

(209)(a)   (i) Peter said *NP*.
           (ii) Peter could never pass the exam.
(209)(b)   (i) Peter said *NP*.
           (ii) He could never pass the exam.

The ambiguous surface structure is derived by replacing *NP* in (i) by the whole of string (ii). (*That* appears simply as a sign that this particular *NP*-replacement transformation has been applied; it adds nothing to the meaning.) Then in the case of (a), a pronominalization

101

transformation substitutes *he* for the second occurrence of *Peter* (assuming that it is co-referential with *Peter* in (a) (i)). From these examples we see that a pronoun may either be introduced in deep structure – case (b) – or, later, by a pronoun transformation – case (a). The distinction can also be seen in (217), (218):

(217)   John stood up for him.
(218)   John stood up for himself.

In (217) the pronoun *him* is introduced in deep structure; in (218) the underlying structure is *John stood up for John,* with the second *John* pronominalized and (obligatorily) reflexivized – the pronoun is not introduced in deep structure.

The distinction between pronouns in deep structure and pronouns introduced by transformation answers to a distinction between two different 'uses' of pro-forms. On the one hand, a pro-form may be used to reduce redundancy – to avoid repeating information which the sentence has already given. This is one sense in which a pro-form can be said to 'stand for' some fully-spelt-out form. In another usage, a pronoun, say, may be used in deep structure to refer to a person, thing or concept which is given by the context and does not need to be fully specified. This usage is found in (205), (210), (215) – *I* – and in (211) – *us* –, (217) – *him* – and possibly (213) – *anyone.*

The representation of pronouns is the same whether they appear in deep structure or not. For simplicity, we will begin with the case where the pronoun is present in underlying structure, as, for example, in the following sentence:

(219)   I am a writer.

The first thing to notice is that *I* is a kind of *NP*, not a kind of *N*. This observation is supported by the unacceptability of sentences with an article or some other pre-modifier placed before the pronoun: **the I . . ., *some I . . ., *two Is. . . .* When a repeated *NP* is pronominalized, the article (etc.) disappears as well as the *N*:

(220)   (*)The builder said that the builder would do the job.
(221)   The builder said that he would do the job.
But not (222) *The builder said that the he would do the job.

It is, of course, quite clear that pronouns are derived from a sequence *Det + N* and not from *N* by itself, because pronouns give information which is characteristically supplied by *N* and, at the same time, information which is the characteristic responsibility of *Det. I* or *he* allows one to say something like *Roger Fowler* or *John* or *builder*: it carries lexical reference. At the same time, deictic information is given: *I* and *he* are [– Pl] and [– Universal]. Thus it is reasonable to suppose that pronouns are developed from a regular branching

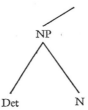

In deep structure, the components of the meaning of a pronoun will be distributed between *Det* and *N* and, later, realization rules will amalgamate these components and render the assembled complex as a single morpheme.

The meaning of *I* (as in (219)) can be represented in this way:

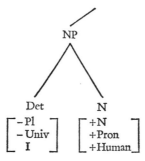

The other pronouns in the system to which *I* belongs appear to be represented as follows:

you (sg.): $\begin{bmatrix} -Pl \\ -Univ \\ II \end{bmatrix} + \begin{bmatrix} +N \\ +Pron \\ +Human \end{bmatrix}$ *you* (pl.): $\begin{bmatrix} +Pl \\ -Univ \\ II \end{bmatrix} + \begin{bmatrix} +N \\ +Pron \\ +Human \end{bmatrix}$

he: $\begin{bmatrix} -Pl \\ -Univ \\ III \end{bmatrix} + \begin{bmatrix} +N \\ +Pron \\ \pm Human \\ +Masc \end{bmatrix}$ *she*: $\begin{bmatrix} -Pl \\ -Univ \\ III \end{bmatrix} + \begin{bmatrix} +N \\ +Pron \\ \pm Human \\ -Masc \end{bmatrix}$

it: $\begin{bmatrix} -Pl \\ -Univ \\ III \end{bmatrix} + \begin{bmatrix} +N \\ +Pron \\ \pm Animate \\ -Human \end{bmatrix}$

we: $\begin{bmatrix} +Pl \\ -Univ \\ I \end{bmatrix} + \begin{bmatrix} +N \\ +Pron \\ +Human \end{bmatrix}$ *they:* $\begin{bmatrix} +Pl \\ -Univ \\ III \end{bmatrix} + \begin{bmatrix} +N \\ +Pron \\ \pm Animate \\ \pm Human \end{bmatrix}$

(This notation does not take account of personification – *Oh! you lakes and mountains!*; or humanization of animals – *You're a good boy, aren't you?* addressed to a dog; or sex-attribution to inanimate objects – *She's a beauty* spoken of a car or boat.)

Notice that the features are divided up between the left (*Det*) and right (*N*) sets according to principles which are entirely compatible with the principles regularly employed in the formation of non-pronominalized *NP*s. In the right-hand set we have features which relate to the semantic nature of nominals: animacy, human-ness, sex; on the left, conventional deictic features, including person, which as we saw in Ch. 6 (p. 62) is a typical deictic dimension. I assume that these features are distributed thus by a sequence of feature-inserting and feature-shifting rules of a familiar kind. A terminal symbol N may be replaced either by a set of features $[+N \ldots +F_n]$, as shown in Ch. 5, or by a set of features $[+N, +Pron \ldots +F_n]$. If the latter option is selected, the set headed $[+N]$ must be further marked in respect of $[\pm Animate]$ and $[\pm Human]$; so in one derivation we might have the successive lines

$$\text{Det} + \begin{bmatrix} +N \\ +\text{Pron} \end{bmatrix} + X$$

$$\text{Det} + \begin{bmatrix} +N \\ +\text{Pron} \\ +\text{Human} \end{bmatrix} + X$$

($[+Human]$ implies $[+Animate]$, which therefore does not have to be marked explicitly in the derivation.)

The next stage involves partial interpretation of *Det*; $[+Pl]$ or $[-Pl]$ may be chosen, but $[-Univ]$ must be chosen. There is, next, an obligatory choice between three manifestations of Person, here shown as $[I/II/III]$. So one possible line is

$$\begin{bmatrix} -\text{Pl} \\ -\text{Univ} \\ I \end{bmatrix} + \begin{bmatrix} +N \\ +\text{Pron} \\ +\text{Human} \end{bmatrix} + X$$

which becomes, of course, *I*. But suppose $[III]$ had been chosen:

$$\begin{bmatrix} -\text{Pl} \\ -\text{Univ} \\ III \end{bmatrix} + \begin{bmatrix} +N \\ +\text{Pron} \\ +\text{Human} \end{bmatrix} + X$$

In that situation, we have to refer back to the $[+N]$ cluster and determine the sex of the referent; so the next line may be

$$\begin{bmatrix} -\text{Pl} \\ -\text{Univ} \\ III \end{bmatrix} + \begin{bmatrix} +N \\ +\text{Pron} \\ +\text{Human} \\ +\text{Masc} \end{bmatrix} + X$$

which is one of the two underlying formulas for *he*. (The other one contains [– Human].) Other pronouns are selected in a similar way, by a sequence of feature-manipulating rules which progressively expand the content of *Det* and *N*, making cross-reference between the two symbols wherever necessary. (An exercise in the development of the other personal pronouns is offered at the end of this chapter.) These transformational operations are followed by a sequence of realization rules designed to turn a pair of fully-developed featuresets into a distinctive morpheme.

These rules are all that are needed to generate pronouns where the pronouns are introduced in deep structure: (219) was our typical example, or (217). Now we turn from pronoun-formation in deep structure to consider *pronominalization*, the process by which a pronoun is substituted for an *NP* which is *not* a pronoun in deep structure. The two distinctive cases to be accounted for are illustrated by (218) and (221):

(218)   John stood up for himself.
(221)   The builder said that he would do the job.

(assuming that *the builder* = *he*). We should also take note of the fact that **The builder said that himself would do the job* is ungrammatical and that *John stood up for him* does not have the same meaning as (218). But (223) is acceptable:

(223)   The builder said that he would stand up for himself.

where *the builder* = *he* = *himself*. Finally, **Himself stood up for John* is ungrammatical.

A basic three-part statement which is the key to these facts of acceptability and unacceptability is this:

(a) Where an *NP* is repeated in the same underlying P-marker, the second occurrence of the *NP* must be replaced by a reflexive pronoun. This makes (218) inevitable since the deep structure is as follows (overleaf) and *John* = *John*:

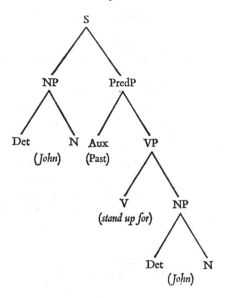

The repeated *NP*s are in the same underlying P-marker.

(b) Where repeated *NP*s are not in the same underlying P-marker, neither the second nor the first *NP* may be replaced by a reflexive pronoun. So *The builder said that himself would do the job* is defined as ungrammatical because it is a complex sentence with the following analysis:

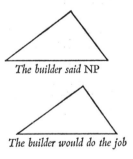

Since the two occurrences of the *NP the builder* are in different underlying P-markers, neither can be replaced by a reflexive pronoun. But of course the second *NP* can be pronominalized.

(c) Where an *NP* is repeated in a different underlying P-marker, it is pronominalized, or, in some circumstances, deleted completely. From the interconnected pair of P-markers drawn under (b) above we must derive (221), because if pronominalization did not occur –

106

The builder said that the builder would do the job – the implication would be that *the builder* ≠ *the builder*. So *The builder said that the builder would do the job* must become *The builder said that he would do the job*; note, however, that this is an ambiguous surface structure, since *he* might have been introduced in deep structure (*he* ≠ *the builder*). Pronominalization takes effect in simple strings after reflexivization, and in situations where subordination (embedding) has applied; when two strings are *conjoined* to make a complex sentence (see Ch. 13), the second occurrence of the repeated *NP* is deleted. So *John runs and John plays football* must become *John runs and plays football* if *John = John*.

In practical analysis based on these observations, it is a prerequisite that we are able to distinguish between simple and complex sentences. In effect, this is no problem, since the base constituent-structure rules automatically make this distinction available. The second crucial factor is the sequence in which pronoun transformations are applied. Our three-part statement can be reduced to two obligatory formal rules which must apply in a fixed order. The *reflexivization rule* comes first (and we must attempt to apply it to all strings):

$$NP + Aux + V + NP' \Rightarrow NP + Aux + V + NP' + \textit{-self}$$

where the input (left) string is the output of the PSG and $NP = NP'$. So

John stood up for John

becomes

John stood up for John + self

After reflexivization, the pronominalization rule *must* apply:

$$X + NP + Y + NP' + Z \Rightarrow X + NP + Y + Pron + Z$$

Where X, Y and Z are anything (and X and Z may be nothing) and $NP = NP'$. Since *John stood up for John + self* is an instance of the input to the pronominalization rule, it is changed to

John stood up for Pron + self

Notice that this pronominalization rule is so framed as to permit application to non-reflexivized structures as well as to those which have undergone the reflexive transformation. That is to say, it accounts for one reading of (221), for example, as well as for (218).

In detail, the effect of the pronominalization rule is to insert the feature [+ Pron] within the *N* of the pronominalized *NP*, at the same time deleting all features which identify *John* particularly:

$$X + NP + Y + Det + \begin{bmatrix} +N \\ +Name \\ +Human \\ \cdot \\ \cdot \\ \cdot \\ +F_n \end{bmatrix} + Z \Rightarrow X + NP + Y + Det + \begin{bmatrix} +N \\ +Pron \\ +Human \end{bmatrix} + Z$$

The pronoun-formation process described on pp. 104–5 above now takes effect to produce a pair of feature-sets underlying *him*. (More accurately, the structure of the nominative *he* is derived and is then, by a separate process, rendered as the accusative *him*; for details, see below, pp. 112–13.)

Let us now see how these rules work in the cases of (221) and (223):

(221)   The builder said that he would do the job.
(223)   The builder said that he would stand up for himself.

As we saw, the constituent structure of (221) has the following analysis:

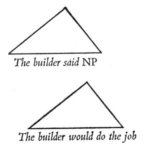

The builder said NP

The builder would do the job

First we attempt to apply the reflexivization rule. As the two occurrences of the repeated *NP* are in different underlying P-markers, this rule cannot apply, so we pass on to pronominalization. We have an instance of a string

X   +   NP   +   Y   +   NP′   +   Z

(*the builder*) (*said*) (*the builder*) (*would do the job*)

so pronominalization can take place to change *NP′* into a pronoun in the manner shown above.

(223) may be diagrammed thus:

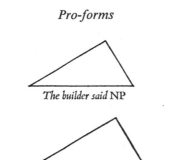

The builder said NP

The builder would stand up for the builder

Again, reflexivization is attempted as a first move. In this case, it can be applied, since the subordinate clause is based on an underlying P-marker which fulfils the conditions for reflexivization: $NP = NP'$ in the same underlying P-marker. The structure becomes

> The builder said (the builder would stand up for the builder + self)

Now pronominalization is operative, and the transformation is applied twice. First, the second *NP* in the subordinate clause is pronominalized:

> The builder said (the builder would stand up for himself)

Then the *NP*s which are repeated across the boundary of the P-markers are processed:

> The builder said that he would stand up for himself.

The derivations sketched for (221) and (223) illustrate two extremely important facts about the mode of application of transformational rules. First, we have seen that the order of application of transformations is crucial. Any variation in the sequence of operations indicated above will result in failure to generate the target sentences. (You may care to test this assertion.) Second, the particular transformations we have investigated, like all T-rules, make close reference to the constituent structure of sentences – they apply to *phrase-markers*, not to unstructured strings of formatives. This fact is dramatically illustrated by pronominalizing derivations. It would be all too easy to regard pronominal substitution as a left-to-right, purely linear arrangement. Of course, pronominal replacement *does* obey linear conditions, for obvious semantic reasons: a full *NP* is more completely specified than its substitute pronoun, and encountering the fully detailed element earlier in the string must aid comprehension. But this result is not achieved by a strictly linear processing: in the case of the derivation for (223), for instance, we saw that tree-structure was a vastly more important control for transformational processing than surface-structure sequence.

Before we leave the subject of pronouns, there are two more topics which deserve brief comment: there are some further facts about reflexives which may be noted, and there is the question of the 'case' of pronouns: how do we distinguish *he* and *him*, and what is the origin of the possessive *his*?

First, some additional observations on reflexives. There is an interesting sub-class of verbs which can occur *only* in reflexive constructions:

$$(224) \quad \text{John} \left\{ \begin{array}{l} \text{expressed} \\ \text{bestirred} \\ \text{behaved} \\ \text{perjured} \\ \text{absented} \end{array} \right\} \text{himself.}$$

These are called *absolute reflexives*. What we have is a type of transitive verb which demands that the Subject-*NP* should be [+ Animate] (and in some cases [+ Human]), and that the Subject-*NP* should be duplicated in the Object. These are highly specific restrictions, and, in the spirit of Ch. 5, the best place to note them is in the lexicon. So the lexical entry for *behave*, for instance, might be written:

$$\begin{bmatrix} +\,V \\ +\_\text{NP} \\ -\,\text{Pass} \\ +\,[\,+\,\text{Animate}]\_ \\ [\,+\,[\_\text{NP} = \text{NP}\_]\,] \\ . \\ . \\ . \\ +\,F_n \end{bmatrix}$$

This entry will ensure that, at the stage of lexical interpretation, *behave* follows only Subjects marked [+ Animate], and that the post-verbal *NP* is identical to the Subject-*NP*. This latter condition will automatically trigger the reflexivization transformation and then the pronominalization transformation.

A quite different kind of phenomenon is offered by *reciprocal reflexives*. The following sentences show that there is a major difference of meaning between *themselves* and *each other/ one another*:

(225)   Mr Smith and Mr Brown thought highly of one another.
(226)   Mr Smith and Mr Brown thought highly of themselves.
(227)   John and Mary met one another at the station.
(228)   *John and Mary met themselves at the station.

(225) means 'Mr Smith thought highly of Mr Brown and Mr Brown thought highly of Mr Smith'; (226) means *either* 'Mr Smith thought highly of himself and Mr Brown thought highly of himself' *or* 'Mr Smith and Mr Brown thought highly of the partnership of Mr Smith and Mr Brown'. A grammar must distinguish all these meanings. Although I do not intend to attempt this differentiation here, let me mention that the discussion of *phrasal conjunction* in Ch. 13 may be relevant to the solution of this problem with reflexives.

Finally, reflexives shed some light on imperatives. The conventional analysis of imperatives is that they are based on a structure *you + PredP* with *you* deleted – in our account, obligatorily deleted by a T-rule triggered by the feature [Imp] selected under *Aux*. If we had only sentences like the following, this analysis would be difficult to justify – how can one say that *you* has been deleted when there is no direct evidence that it was ever present? This difficulty completely inhibited treatment of imperatives in pre-transformational grammars, which refused to admit that sentences like these had a deleted or 'understood' *you* as Subject:

(229)   Go away.
(230)   Shut the door.

But certain restrictions on reflexive imperatives seem to justify our analysis:

(231)   *Defend itself.
(232)   *Help himself.
(233)   Defend yourself.
(234)   Help yourself.

Apparently, reflexive imperatives can be based only on a structure containing *you* in the Object-*NP*. According to our analysis of reflexives, *yourself* is based on a *you* repeated from the Subject-*NP*. The underlying structure of (233) must be *you defend you*; reflexivization, pronominalization and then the imperative transformation must be the main stages in its derivational history. (Note that, once again, order of T-rules is vital: the imperative must be formed after the reflexive, because if deletion of Subject took place first, reflexivization would be impossible.) Analogously, *Help himself* must be based on *he helps him*, with an intermediate stage *he helps himself*. What prevents the imperative transformation being applied to this intermediate string? The only possible answer is: the presence of the feature [III] in the Subject-*NP*, since that is the only respect in which the Subjects of *you defend yourself* and *he helps himself* differ. Other comparative material establishes that the imperative transformation can take place only when [II] is present in the Subject of a sentence.

The second 'left-over' topic in this chapter concerns what is called *case*. In English there is variation between *I/me/my, he/him/his, she/her/her, it/it/its, we/us/our, you/you/your* and *they/them/their*. One form of the pronoun rather than another is selected depending on the function of the pronoun in syntactic structure; in many other languages, case is a property of nouns as well as pronouns, but in English only pronouns are affected except where the possessive case is concerned:

(235)   He left the room.
(236)   The police caught him.
(237)   Mr Jones has sold his house.

The *possessive case*, illustrated in (237) and in (238) below, is a rather separate matter:

(238)   The estate agent sold Mr Jones's house.

Possessives appear to be derived from underlying strings with *have* used as a transitive verb. On this analysis, both (237) and (238) are complex sentences, that is, they imply two underlying strings each:

(237)   (a)   Mr Jones has sold *NP*
        (b)   Mr Jones has a house.
(238)   (a)   The estate agent sold *NP*
        (b)   Mr Jones had a house.

(Note that tense is consistent in the pairs of underlying strings.) In each case, a multi-part transformation 'nominalizes' (b) to *Mr Jones's house*; then this *NP* is substituted for the unspecified *NP* in (a). The amalgamation of (237) (a) and (b) leads to a repeated *NP*, and thus to pronominalization – but since the two occurrences of *Mr Jones* are not in the same underlying P-marker, reflexivization cannot apply to produce **Mr Jones has sold himself's house*. Pronominalization is irrelevant to (238), of course.

For the origin of another type of possessive, see Ch. 11, p. 130.

The difference between (235) and (236) is best shown by a feature analysis. *Him* in (236) is traditionally called *accusative* case, so let us assign it a feature [+ Acc]. *He* will be [– Acc] (traditionally 'nominative'), but there is probably no need to mark it so. Now the *him* of (236) is a deep-structure pronoun, just like the *he* of (235), and there is no reason to believe that they do not have the same underlying representation; this representation is neutral as to [±Acc]:

$$
\begin{bmatrix} -\text{Pl} \\ -\text{Univ} \\ \text{III} \end{bmatrix} + \begin{bmatrix} +\text{N} \\ +\text{Pron} \\ \pm\text{Human} \\ +\text{Masc} \end{bmatrix}
$$

Supposing that *he* and *him* in these two examples are both [+ Human], the following simplified representations of the strings in which they occur would be appropriate:

(235)
$$
\begin{bmatrix} -\text{Pl} \\ -\text{Univ} \\ \text{III} \end{bmatrix} + \begin{bmatrix} +\text{N} \\ +\text{Pron} \\ +\text{Human} \\ +\text{Masc} \end{bmatrix} + \text{Aux} + \text{X}
$$

(236)
$$
\text{Y} + \text{V} + \begin{bmatrix} -\text{Pl} \\ -\text{Univ} \\ \text{III} \end{bmatrix} + \begin{bmatrix} +\text{N} \\ +\text{Pron} \\ +\text{Human} \\ +\text{Masc} \end{bmatrix}
$$

Several other sentences or strings cited in this chapter, including, for example, (218) and (224), have the same representation as (236), and the same rule will inflect the Object Pronouns in all of them for accusative case:

$$
\text{Y} + \text{V} + \begin{bmatrix} \text{Number} \\ -\text{Univ} \\ \text{Person} \end{bmatrix} + \begin{bmatrix} +\text{N} \\ +\text{Pron} \\ \pm\text{Animate} \\ \pm\text{Human} \end{bmatrix} \Rightarrow \text{Y} + \text{V} + \begin{bmatrix} \text{Number} \\ -\text{Univ} \\ \text{Person} \\ +\text{Acc} \end{bmatrix} + \begin{bmatrix} +\text{N} \\ +\text{Pron} \\ \pm\text{Animate} \\ \pm\text{Human} \end{bmatrix}
$$

The feature [+ Acc] is assigned to the *Det*-complex of a pronominalized *NP* in Object position, and becomes a signal for morphological marking of accusative case in surface structure. This rule ensures that all pronouns in Object position are realized as accusative, and that no pronouns in any other position receive that realization.

Exercises and topics for discussion

1. Give a careful definition of the concept 'pro-form'.
2. Compile a classified list, more extensive than (204)–(215), of sentences containing various kinds of pro-forms.
3. Investigate some possible ways of formalizing the notion of 'co-reference'. Why is this notion essential to an account of pro-formation?
4. Chapter 9 has dealt only with definite pronouns. What indefinite pronouns would a grammar of English need to describe?

5. Discuss the syntactic implications of *personification*.

6. Show how feature-developing transformations are responsible for the descriptions of personal pronouns given on p. 103 above. (The derivations of *I* and *he* are illustrated in the text.)

7. Describe the origins of the personal and reflexive pronouns in the following sentences. Draw trees for surface structure where necessary.

    (a) I have eaten my dinner.
    (b) The bridesmaids promised they would behave themselves.
    (c) The woman who identified the burglar claimed that he had forced his way into her house.
    (d) The chairman ignored us.
    (e) Her father said that Mary had surpassed herself.

8. Explain the unacceptability of the following sentences:

    (a) *Himself protects Mr Smith.
    (b) *Himself laughs.
    (c) *Amuse oneself.
    (d) *He is gifted and Peter should go far. (*He* = *Peter*)
    (e) *I told him to protect myself.
    (f) *Her left the door unlocked.
    (g) *I see me.

9. Explain the ambiguity of the following sentences:

    (a) Mary's mother said that she had disgraced herself.
    (b) Mr Brown claimed that he had left the party before midnight.
    (c) Mary and John condemned themselves.
    (d) When Tom shook hands with him he was very nervous.

ten

Complex Sentences

We have now surveyed a wide range of aspects of English structure, and it may be useful to take stock of the position we have reached, before extending this survey. At the outset I claimed that the responsibility of a grammarian is to assign structural descriptions to sentences: to the infinite set of well-formed sentences which constitutes a natural language. This responsibility is to be discharged in a manner consistent with an overall psychological criterion: the grammarian must describe sentences in such a way as to account for what mature speakers know about those sentences. All relevant facts about synonymy, ambiguity, grammaticalness and structure must be provided, since these define areas of tacit linguistic knowledge which, to judge by their linguistic behaviour and intuitions, speakers must possess. Bearing this criterion and others in mind, we arrived at a definition of generative grammar. Moving on from that point, I indicated that a kind of generative grammar which seems to perform these tasks particularly well is a transformational grammar – a grammar which, from a general point of view, can be defined as one which recognizes a deep structure/surface structure distinction in syntax; and from a more specific viewpoint, one which employs certain formally distinctive kinds of linguistic rule. A transformational grammar is for several reasons a most efficient kind of generative grammar. There are many structural details of natural language which only transformations can describe really adequately: discontinuous structure, sentence-relationships, certain kinds of ambiguity, and so on. Again, the general theory of deep structure is a substantial contribution to our understanding of the problem of sound-meaning relations. Most of all, perhaps, the advantage of a TG is that it performs its descriptive duties in a formal and very explicit manner, and thus is open to exact discussion and justification (or, just as important, disproof).

Chapters 3 to 8 have examined the most important, indeed indispensable, concepts in linguistic analysis: the difference between constituent structure and transformational structure, the basic syntactic functions, the design of a scheme of lexical categories; the development of abstract syntactic frames – structured phrase-markers – to accommodate both the semantic content of propositions and the information which 'orientates' sentences in relation to the non-linguistic world; the presentation of dictionary entries, and the use of dictionary ʹentries relative to syntax; the role of transformational rules in inserting, deleting and amalgamating morphemes and features on the basis of an abstract, simple, pre-transformational sub-structure. I have presented this information in such a way that the reader has been shown how to construct derivations. As we have seen, 'derivation' is an important concept in linguistic theory. But of more immediate importance is its practical, analytic, function: it is the device by which one assigns a structural description to a real sentence. A derivation is a route between S and some grammatical sentence of L; following that route, one invokes certain rules in a certain order. If the rules are correctly stated, the process of derivation shows that we are dealing with a sentence of L, and a particular sentence of L; we are able to relate that sentence to S and to L in a principled way.

In the process of reviewing these general notions, and of formalizing the technique of derivation, we have considered a variety of English sentences: statements, different sorts of question, negatives, passives, various Aspects and Moods, sentences containing pronouns, sentences with and without Objects, and so on. By now, the reader has enough information to allow him to attach structural descriptions to many thousands of English sentences. But there has been one major limitation: although all the sentences have involved transformational processing, and although these processes have been, formally speaking, quite complicated – the rules for expanding *Det* come to mind – most of the sentences discussed so far have been, in the technical sense, *simple*. A simple sentence, it will be remembered, is one which is based on only one underlying P-marker: it begins from one and only one S. A moment's thought establishes two facts about the potential corpus of such sentences. First, they are rather rare in actual discourse – a look at the text of any page of this book will reveal that natural sentences are usually much longer and more complicated than the simple sentences of our examples. Second, there are obvious limitations on the *size* of the corpus of simple sentences. Even if there are 'many thousands' in English, the absolute number will be strictly limited – a straightforward product of the size of the vocabulary, the selectional restrictions obtaining between individual lexical items, and the range of structural combinations allowed by the rules on which we have focused.

To account for the range and creativity of the set of sentences of any natural language, we need only to supplement the notion of simple sentences with a definition of *complex* sentences: these are, of course, sentences which are based on more than one underlying P-marker, sentences whose derivations begin with two or more separate *S*s. Up to now we have perhaps assumed that the natural thing to do with an underlying phrase-marker is to flesh it out and let it see the light of day as a simple sentence. Actually, such P-markers are more typically components of complex sentences than sole bases for simple sentences.

Complex sentences are an enormous benefit in linguistic description. Immediately we can put strings together, we can introduce variety and infinite potentiality into the set of sentences which defines *L*. Variety arises because underlying strings can be put together in many different ways:

(239)   I went to the window and looked out.
(240)   Going to the window, I looked out.
(241)   I looked out after going to the window.
(242)   I went to the window, then looked out.
(243)   After I went to the window, I looked out.

Infinite potentiality is a property of a syntax with complex sentences because some combinations of strings are indefinitely extensible (a point which was illustrated in Ch. 1):

(244)   John eats meat, vegetables, bread . . . and fruit.
(245)   John believed that Mary claimed that Peter maintained that . . .
(246)   This hot, dry, sunny, lazy, predictable . . . climate suits me very well.

Each of these sentences can be made longer, without limit, by the reapplication of a transformational rule which adds one more underlying string. So (244) is based on the strings *John eats meat, John eats vegetables, John eats bread, John eats fruit*; we can readily add *John eats soup, John eats cheese*, etc. We do not need a new rule to extend the sentence each time: just one complex-sentence-forming rule can be applied over and over again. Such a rule is called a *recursive* rule, and recursiveness is a property of complex sentences.

(Note: the present model of syntax attributes recursive qualities to the transformational section, as in *Syntactic Structures*. The model of syntax offered by Katz & Postal's *Integrated Theory of Linguistic Descriptions* and by Chomsky's *Aspects of the Theory of Syntax* proposes a base grammar with recursive power. Readers will find it illuminating to compare the techniques and motivations of these several interpretations by studying the primary sources concerned.)

Recursiveness is an exceedingly powerful economy in syntax, and the possibility of recursive rules is one of the primary justifications for a transformational level of analysis in syntax. (246) will illustrate this claim. In the present account, we treat (246) as a complex sentence: it is based on a 'main clause' *This climate suits me very well* and a number of 'subordinate clauses' *This climate is hot, This climate is sunny,* etc. To generate this sentence, we need whatever rules are required to generate each underlying string, plus one rule which will combine the strings: the economy is that only one rule (actually, one sequence of rules, but that does not affect the argument) is needed to put the adjectives in prenominal position – preceding *climate*. This same rule is applied as many times as there are subordinate strings to be reduced to prenominal adjectives. In effect, only one rule is required to extend a sentence to any length. Thus the phenomenon 'no longest sentence' is accounted for by a finite number of rules. This is not the case in a non-transformational approach. Supposing that we treated (246) as a simple sentence, we would be obliged to account for its constituent structure by a set of rewriting rules:

$$\text{NP} \rightarrow \text{Det} + \begin{cases} \text{Adj} + \text{N} \\ \text{Adj} + \text{Adj} + \text{N} \\ \text{Adj} + \text{Adj} + \text{Adj} + \text{N} \\ \text{Adj} + \text{Adj} + \text{Adj} + \text{Adj} + \text{N} \\ \text{Adj} + \text{Adj} + \text{Adj} + \text{Adj} + \text{Adj} + \text{N} \end{cases}$$

As it stands, (246) contains only five preposed adjectives, so the above rule is adequate; but a sentence of this type can be lengthened without apparent limit, so more rules must be proposed:

$$\text{NP} \rightarrow \text{Det} + \begin{cases} \text{Adj} + \text{Adj} + \text{Adj} + \text{Adj} + \text{Adj} + \text{Adj} + \text{N} \\ \text{Adj} + \text{Adj} + \text{Adj} + \text{Adj} + \text{Adj} + \text{Adj} + \text{Adj} + \text{N} \\ \text{etc.} \end{cases}$$

Evidently, on this analysis we would need as many rewriting rules as there are adjectives before the noun – in fact, an indefinite number. By comparison with the reapplicable (recursive) rule facility, this is obviously extremely wasteful; there are also more compelling reasons why we should reject an analysis by rewriting rules of this kind of construction. A grammar with mentalistic pretensions – one which claims to represent speakers' internalized knowledge of their language – must be finite: it must contain a determinate number of rules. A human being is a finite organism: therefore it is impossible that such an organism could acquire any knowledge which had to be represented in a non-finite set of rules. If we intend a grammar to tell us something about linguistic competence, we must not let the grammar enshrine a psychologically falsifiable principle.

Even if we were not impressed with this latter, psychological, argument, we would still be left with the fact that a transformational grammar with recursive rules represents a substantial gain in economy over other alternatives. In the case of our particular example (246), we may say that treating this as a complex sentence, rather than as a simple sentence to be accounted for by the PSG, has the effect of simplifying the grammar quite considerably. I point this out partly as a comfort to readers. It would be wrong to expect that since the account of simple sentences in Chs. 3 to 9 has been rather demanding, complex sentences, to which we now turn, must in the nature of the case be inconceivably more difficult to analyse. In fact, the most difficult transformations have already been dealt with, transformations which are complicated whether they contribute to technically 'simple' or technically 'complex' sentences. The economy of complex sentence-formation is so great that, once we have learnt to generate simple sentences, we can go on to explain how they are combined into very much more intricate constructions with a disproportionately small increase of complexity in the mechanics of rule-writing.

Towards the end of Ch. 9 I began to employ the traditional terminology of 'main clauses' versus 'subordinate clauses'. This tactic was intended to bring home the point that a change in the structural materials treated by this book was about to occur. The sentence in question, (223), was virtually a classic example of the 'complex sentence' in traditional grammar:

(223)   The builder said that he would stand up for himself.

In the older 'school grammar', this would have been said to consist of a main clause *The builder said* and a subordinate clause *that he would stand up for himself*. Note that these clauses can be readily separated from one another and from the whole sentence. On such kinds of sentence, the analyses of TG and of traditional grammar tend to coincide, except that traditional grammar would derive (223) from two 'sentences' and TG from two abstract 'underlying phrase-markers'. As we shall see, there are several other types of complex sentence which receive parallel analyses in the conventional and the contemporary modes (cf. (245)). But (244) and (246) are also treated as complex sentences by transformational grammarians, and they do not display a sequence of easily segmentable 'clauses'. The distance between TG and conventional syntactic analysis on this issue may be emphasized by the following list of what are complex sentences in the present treatment, some of which are nothing of the kind under the older scheme; for clarity, in some cases I have italicized material which has been introduced from secondary strings:

(247) John came but Bill didn't.
(248) Looking back over the year, we can feel satisfied.
(249) I'll do it when I get home.
(250) I went out and had a meal.
(251) I can't come because I have no money.
(252) The man who bought the car gave a *false* address.
(253) That he has escaped is regrettable.
(254) They would like *Peter to go*.
(255) They would like *to go*.
(256) *To give in* would be a mistake.
(257) *Cooking* is boring.
(258) John *or Bill* will oblige.
(259) Two men *from Mexico* crossed the frontier.
(260) Two *Mexican* labourers crossed the frontier.
(261) *Her* mother helped her.
(262) He was sleeping *peacefully*.

Several of these sentences are obviously complex: the separate underlying strings are kept distinct in surface structure. This is especially evident in (247)–(253), except for *false* in (252), which represents a subordinate string. Then, if we accept that underlying strings may be substantially modified by the transformational processes which join them together, (254)–(258) can also be recognized as complex. But the italicized words in (259)–(262), and *false* in (252), are severely reduced reflexes of underlying strings, and it is probably for this reason that grammarians working without a transformational apparatus have not regarded sentences containing such constituents as complex. Nevertheless, the italicized elements can be shown convincingly to be abbreviated realizations of full underlying strings: *the address was false* for (252), *She had a mother* for (261), etc. It is true that some rather complicated rules are needed to derive these structures in their heavily modified surface forms, but this is only to be expected, given the superficial diversity of the sentences of natural languages; and the deviousness of the transformational component is more than compensated for by the simplicity and power of the base grammar which are gained by accounting for such sentences in this way. And if the transformations concerned appear 'devious', they still work in regular, patterned ways and explain a vast number of sentences by a small number of rules, however complicated each rule may be.

Two general distinctions of types of transformation must be made. Transformations were used plentifully to generate simple sentences in the early chapters of this book, but they were mostly of one basic type: each T-rule accepted as its input a single string associated with a P-marker, and changed the characteristics of the string, by re-ordering, insertion or deletion of a feature or a morpheme, and so on. A T-rule which has only one string as input is called a *singulary transformation*. Such a transformation might be pictured as a process $A \Rightarrow B$, where B is an altered version of A. The transformations which we are now about to look at, on the other hand, accept two strings simultaneously as their input, and amalgamate them to derive a new, complex, string: $A + B \Rightarrow C$. Such rules are called *double-base* or *generalized* transformations. As an example, one elementary double-base transformation produces the following result:

A John plays the piano ⎞⇒C John plays the piano and Mary
B Mary sings   ⎠   sings.

Or, with greater disturbance to surface structure, we have

A John will oblige ⎞⇒C John or Bill will oblige.
B Bill will oblige ⎠

(In the above examples, I have given the underlying strings in conventional spelling; these are not, of course, real sentences, but underlying P-markers.)

There is a further important typological distinction, this time between two kinds of generalized transformation. In (263) two underlying strings have been linked in such a way that they retain equivalent status:

(263)   John plays the piano and Mary sings.

There is no way of saying which of the two linked statements – *John plays the piano* or *Mary sings* – is the dominant one. The situation may be diagrammed thus:

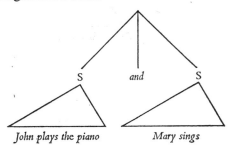

121

One could reverse the superficial order without altering the deep structure or the meaning:

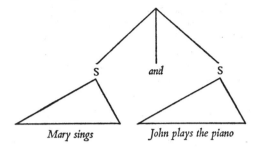

Mary sings   John plays the piano

Traditional grammar recognizes this type of construction, in which all underlying strings are syntactically of equal rank, by saying that, for instance, (263) consists of two *co-ordinated clauses*. In TG we say that (263) is a *conjoined* construction, that the two underlying strings are brought together by a conjoining or conjunction transformation. (258), *John or Bill will oblige*, is another example of conjoining, as are (247), (250), and, perhaps, (248), although in the last case it might be argued that the string *we can feel satisfied* has logical priority over *we look back over the year.*

The other complex sentences in our list are derived by a different kind of rule, as can be seen by comparing the shape of the above tree-diagrams with the following:

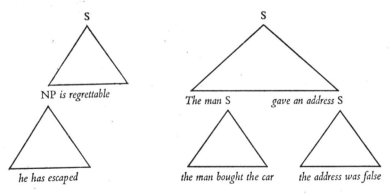

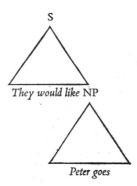

In these complex sentences, and others in the list – although for some of them the fact cannot be easily shown in a tree-diagram – one basic string clearly overshadows the other(s). In (252), the basic statement is about a man giving an address; that the man had bought a car and that the address was false are supplementary or subsidiary statements. This distinction between main and subsidiary statement is shown in tree-diagrams (the main statement always occurs higher up in the tree) and is recognized by the traditional terminological distinction between main and subordinate clauses. Transformational grammar rewords this as *matrix* versus *constituent,* and the relationship between these two ranks of underlying string is said to be a relationship of *embedding.* So in (253), for instance, the constituent string *he has escaped* is embedded as the *NP* of the matrix *NP is regrettable.* An embedding transformation substitutes an *S* for some component of a matrix (e.g. for the *NP* of (253) and (254)) or attaches an *S* to a component of a matrix – as *S* is attached to both the Subject- and Object-*NP*s of the matrix of (252).

So far, our examples have not shown one possibility in the embedding process. 'Matrix' and 'constituent' are not absolute terms, but are only significant when underlying P-markers are in an embedding relationship one with another. So one *S* may be at the same time a constituent of another *S* and matrix for a third *S*. This situation is illustrated in (264), where the middle string is simultaneously a constituent of the top one and a matrix for the lower one:

(264)   They wanted Peter to promise that he would be careful.

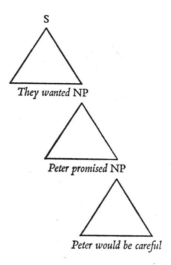

S

They wanted NP

Peter promised NP

Peter would be careful

A second fact about generalized T-rules that has to be noticed is that they apply in a strict sequence, not throwing together all the underlying strings at once but amalgamating P-markers in a set order. We can use the simplified notation introduced on p. 121 above to show this:

A_1 They wanted NP $\quad\Big)\Rightarrow C_1$ They wanted Peter to promise
B_1 Peter promised NP $\quad\Big/\quad$ NP

A_2 They wanted Peter to promise NP $\quad\Big)\Rightarrow C_2$ They wanted Peter
B_2 Peter would be careful NP $\qquad\qquad\Big/\qquad$ to promise that he
$\qquad\qquad\qquad\qquad\qquad\qquad\qquad\qquad\qquad$ would be careful.

Notice that, in the course of this derivation, the active transformations make appropriate morphological adjustments to the constituent strings – deleting *Aux* and supplying *to* in $A_1 + B_1 \Rightarrow C_1$, inserting *that* when A_2 and B_2 are amalgamated. Also, notice that some singulary transformations must be applied at certain set stages of the transformational cycle: here, for instance, pronominalization must occur immediately after A_2 and B_2 have been amalgamated, and not before this amalgamation.

Embedding and conjoining transformations, employed in the ways indicated above, yield a vast range of complex sentences. To conclude this chapter I will refer to some recognizably distinct types of surface structure for which these processes are responsible. The most primitive structure in complex sentences is *multiple branching*. In this arrangement we find a sequence of strings, or words representing reduced strings, with no hierarchical structure:

(265)   John emptied the ashtrays, Clive collected the glasses, Mary washed the dishes and Peter threw out the bottles.

This has a linear structure

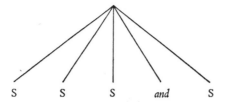

(266) is a multiple-branching surface structure based on reduced strings:

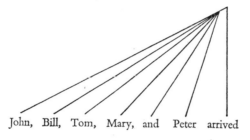

This differs from (265) in that there is hierarchical structure above the multiple-branched *NP*.

There is also *left-branching*, in which modifying elements restrict each other's meaning in a right-left dimension:

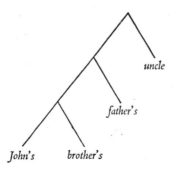

We can see how the reference of *uncle* is progressively delimited as

125

one moves from right to left down the branches of the tree. A *right-branching* version of this would be

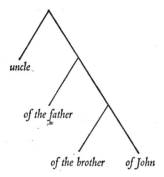

Another important type of right-branching is represented by sentences of the *The house that Jack built* variety:

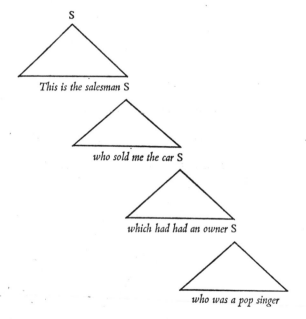

A most valuable quality of multiple-branching, left-branching and right-branching constructions is that they are recursive, and so contribute to the boundlessness of the corpus of English sentences. Furthermore, they may be, and characteristically are, combined in

many ways to introduce great variety into the superficial structure of complex sentences:

(267) John, his beautiful girlfriend Mary, shy old Peter and a woman from Hampstead all arrived at the same time.

(268) Two students whom I knew vaguely and who said they were friends of my son came and sang protest songs.

Two more types of complex superficial structure that we should recognize are *nesting* and *self-embedding*. A nested construction is one which is totally enclosed within a matrix. In (269), *who bought the car* is nested but *which was false* is not – there is no part of the matrix to the right of it:

(269) The man who bought the car gave an address which was false.

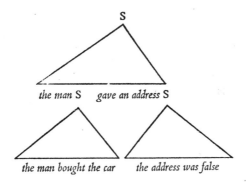

Finally, some nested constructions are also self-embedded. A self-embedded construction is one which is totally enclosed (nested) within a construction *of the same type*. In (270), the italicized string is self-embedded within the string printed in heavy type:

(270) The book **which the professor** *whom the students respected* **recommended** was out of print.

Self-embedding carries with it an immediate problem: sentences which have this characteristic can be extremely difficult to understand, especially in speech. There are, evidently, some sentences which, though perfectly grammatical, are so complicated as to be psycholinguistically unacceptable. But that kind of unacceptability is outside the subject of the present book.

Exercises and topics for discussion

1. Draw tree-diagrams to show the surface structure of sentences (267), (268) and (270).
2. Collect and analyse some further examples of right-branching and left-branching constructions.
3. Why is it particularly 'economical' to have a distinction between simple and complex sentences of the kind drawn in Ch. 10?
4. What underlying strings are implied by each of the complex sentences (247)–(262)?
5. Illustrate as many different types of conjoining as you can.
6. Define the following terms:

    (a) hierarchical structure
    (b) dominate
    (c) terminal symbol
    (d) singulary transformation
    (e) syntactic feature
    (f) morpheme
    (g) case
    (h) article
    (i) mood
    (j) predicate

eleven

Some Nominalizations

One of the most prolific mechanisms for forming complex sentences is *nominalization*. Many of our examples have involved nominalization, particularly (252)–(257), which for ease of reference I will repeat here:

(252) The man who bought the car gave a false address.
(253) That he has escaped is regrettable.
(254) They would like Peter to go.
(255) They would like to go.
(256) To give in would be a mistake.
(257) Cooking is boring.

Nominalization is an embedding process whereby a sentence-like string is attached to or replaces an *NP*. So in (252), a constituent string *the man bought the car* has been attached to the Subject-*NP the man* of the matrix, and a constituent *the address was false* has been attached to the Object-*NP* of the matrix, *an address*. Both of these constituents have been reduced to appropriate sequences of morphemes before being positioned in surface structure. Adjectives and relative clauses, as illustrated in (252), are such an important class of nominalizations that I devote the whole of Ch. 12 to the part they play in English structure. (253) exemplifies the type of nominal with which we are most concerned in this chapter: the nominalized sentence appears to take over completely the job of the Subject-*NP* of the matrix; the following diagram of this sentence gives a little more information about its surface structure than was provided on p. 122 above:

129

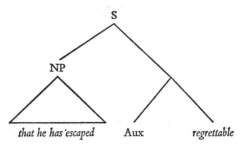

Another version of (253) is

(271)   It is regrettable that he has escaped.

Where does the *it* come from? Shortly I will examine this question;
it will turn out to be crucial to our interpretation of this typical kind
of nominalization.

First, however, consider some examples of another type of
nominal:

(272)   The defeat of the Nazis delighted the nation.
(273)   His collapse demoralized the team.
(274)   The applause of the audience thrilled the cast.
(275)   An employee must be loyal to the firm.
(276)   An employer must be generous to his staff.
(277)   His driving terrifies me.

None of these is a simple sentence. The complexity is obvious in the
case of (277), which is an ambiguous surface structure: the Subject-
NP means either *the way he drives* or *the fact that he drives*, and both
the Subject-*NP* of (277) and these two paraphrases appear to be
nominalizations of *he drives*, parallel to the nominalization of *he has
escaped* found in (253). Most transformationalists would claim that
defeat, collapse, applause, employee and *employer* are relics of similar
processes. We would say that *his collapse* in (273), for instance, does
not imply an underlying noun *collapse* – it is different from, for
example, *his house* (cf. p. 112 above); rather, it is nominalized from
the underlying string *he collapsed*. One advantage of this analysis is
that we economize on lexical entries: it is not necessary to enter
collapse twice, once marked [+V] and once [+N]. There is an added
bonus with (272): we do not need to account for this kind of prepositional phrase, at least (*of the Nazis*), in the base syntax. We are
also able to explain the syntactic difference between (272) and, say,

(278)   The collapse of the Nazis delighted the nation.

The superficial similarity in the sequence *Article-Noun-of-NP* conceals the fact that *the Nazis* is the Object of *defeat* in (272), the Subject of *collapse* in (278). An explanation in terms of nominalization reveals this difference:

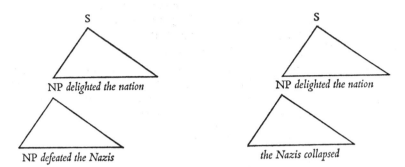

(In a similar way, the ambiguity of a sentence like *His betrayal angered me* would be explained.) Finally, this exposition satisfies our intuition that the difference between the words *employer* and *employee* is primarily syntactic, not semantic. In (275) the referent of the Subject-*NP* is the Object of an underlying verb *employ* (*employee*: *NP employs him*); in (276) it is the Subject of *employ* (*employer*: *he employs NP*). Again the lexical benefit is considerable, since, given adequate morphological (realization) rules, we need enter only *employ* [+ V] in the dictionary, and not *employee* or *employer*. This is not the place to investigate this phenomenon in detail, but it is worth pointing out that a substantial number of what are usually called nouns may be derived from underlying verbs in this way. In particular, nominalization is a natural explanation for the many thousands of words, relatively recent additions to our vocabulary, which end in -(*a*)*tion*, -(*i*)*bility*, etc.

Returning to the nominalizations which are more obvious in superficial syntax – the kind of thing represented by (253) – it may be instructive to compare one example with another sentence which has a similar surface structure but a quite different structural description. The following sentences both involve nominalization, but it is only the first which concerns us for the moment (the second represents a special type which is dealt with in Ch. 12):

(279)   The idea that he was a linguist surprised us.
(280)   The idea that he presented surprised us.

That these sentences have different *SD*s is suggested by some transformational modifications:

(279) (a) It surprised us that he was a linguist.
(280) (a) *It surprised us that he presented.
(279) (b) That he was a linguist was the idea which surprised us.
(280) (b) *That he presented was the idea which surprised us.
(279) (c) We were surprised that he was a linguist.
(280) (c) *We were surprised that he presented.
(279) (d) His being a linguist surprised us.
(280) (d) *His presenting surprised us.

Immediately we recognize a distinction between two quite separate *thats*. Traditionally, *that* in (280) is a relative pronoun, whereas *that* in (279) might be called, rather unrevealingly, a subordinating conjunction. This distinction is underscored by the following contrast:

(281) The idea which he presented surprised us.
(282) *The idea which he was a linguist surprised us.

Since *that* in (280) is a relative pronoun, it can be replaced by *which*; *that* in (279) is not a relative pronoun, so this substitution is impossible. In fact, the constituents *that he was a linguist* and *that he presented* are quite dissimilar, as we can see if we represent the deep structures of (279), (280) thus:

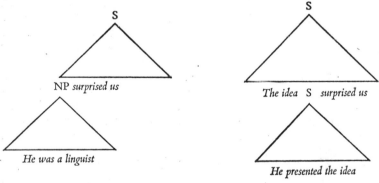

In (280) *idea* is a significant lexical item, the Object of *presented*, and *that* replaces *idea* in the relative clause when it is embedded: (280) is about an idea. (279) is not about an idea, but about the fact of being a linguist (or not being a linguist!); *the idea that* seems to be just one of the several alternative introductory formulas available for embedding *he was a linguist* in the matrix. The nominalization involved in (279) makes the constituent sentence a *noun phrase complement*; (280) nominalizes the constituent as a relative clause.

To judge from superficial structure, it would appear that some sentences functioning as noun phrase complements occupy the whole of an *NP* position in the matrix sentence:

(283) *That he was a linguist* surprised us.
(284) He said *that he was a linguist.*
(285) He said *he was a linguist.*

Comparison of (284) and (285) shows that *that* is not essential to this complementation structure, so apparently the following trees will represent (283) and (284), (285) adequately:

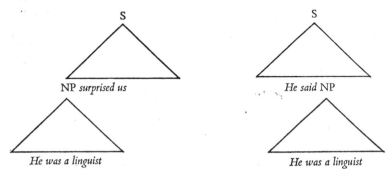

But (283) is synonymous with (286), which contains *it*:

(286) It surprised us that he was a linguist.

It seems that the correct analysis of (283) is not as shown above, but rather

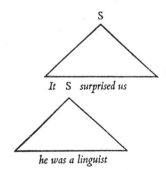

This analysis serves for (286) also, as we shall see.

Turning back to (253), we may suggest that this complex sentence is based on

It – he has escaped – is regrettable

while (279) must be reanalysed as

The idea – he was a linguist – surprised us.

133

Noun phrase complementation, it now seems, is a process by which a constituent *S* is *attached to* an *NP* in the matrix, not *substituted for* it. The *NP* to which a nominalized *S* is attached must be *it*, or one of a small set of formulaic *NP*s such as *the idea, the fact, the claim, the way*, etc. Unlike the *NP*s to which relative clauses are attached (e.g. *the idea* in (280)), these are semantically empty and may readily be deleted. The justification for this analysis – postulating obligatory deletion of *it* in many sentences – is that this is the most satisfactory way of explaining the synonymy of (283) and (286) and of many other such pairs. This solution avoids an awkward special insertion of *it* in such sentences as (286).

Let us now see how this analysis works in a derivation. If we begin with the two underlying strings *It surprised us* (matrix) and *He was a linguist* (constituent), we can derive a number of separate noun phrase complement constructions, using a sequence of transformations. The actual embedding process occurs first, attaching the constituent to the Subject-*NP* of the matrix (for (284), (285) the constituent is attached to the Object):

It – he was a linguist – surprised us.

We now choose what kind of nominal is required: in this case it is a *factive* nominal (see below) which is to be realized as a *that*-form; other possibilities include, for example, the construction underlying *his being a linguist*. In the present derivation we have the intermediate string

It – that he was a linguist – surprised us.

Now this string underlies both (283) and (286). If the target sentence is (286), what is called the *extraposition transformation* is applied, shifting the constituent to the end of the sentence but leaving the *it* at the beginning:

It surprised us – that he was a linguist.

Extraposition has taken place also in the derivations of (271) (p. 130 above) and of several other sentences in the text as well as the illustrations of this chapter. (You may care to look for them.) Extraposition is a regular and productive process in English syntax. But it does not apply in the case of (283); instead, another transformation applies which is obligatory if extraposition does not occur, a transformation called *It-deletion*; so our string

It – that he was a linguist – surprised us

becomes

That he was a linguist – surprised us.

134

Notice that the rule is *It-deletion*, not *NP-deletion*. If the relevant *NP* in the matrix is *the idea, the fact*, etc., deletion does not take place, as we saw from the survival of *the idea* in (279):

The idea that he was a linguist surprised us.

Nor, apparently, may extraposition take place, judging by the oddity of sentences like

(287) (?*) The idea surprised us that he was a linguist.
(288) (?*) The idea appalled us that we might have been in danger of losing our lives.

(288) seems more acceptable than (287). Perhaps the length of the embedded string, and the fact that *Aux* is in a different Mood from that of *appalled*, favour its suspension to the end of the sentence, for ease of processing: *The idea that we might have been in danger of losing our lives appalled us* may be more difficult to understand – when heard rather than read – than the perhaps ungrammatical (288). It is difficult to know what a grammar should do about such facts about usage as these.

At the second stage of our derivation of (283)/(286), a choice of nominals was available. There are nominals with different meanings, and nominals with morphological markers other than *that*:

(256) *To give in* would be a mistake.
(257) *Cooking* is boring.
(283) *That he was a linguist* surprised us.

These three varieties of noun phrase complements do not have the same functions, nor the same distributions – although it must be admitted that the distribution of these forms cannot be stated with any great confidence since their permissibility in certain contexts varies from dialect to dialect. Bearing this qualification in mind, we can still detect some clear differences of function between the three kinds of nominals – those which take *that*, those which use a possessive morpheme and *-ing*, and those which employ the 'in-finitive' form with *to* or, in some dialects, *for to*. *That*-nominals have been aptly called *factive* nominals: typically, they may optionally replace the normally deleted deep structure *it* by *NP*s such as *the fact, the claim, the suggestion*, etc. – thus a characteristic factive nominal might be illustrated by a sentence such as

(289) He acknowledged the fact that the ring had been lost.

In contrast to factive nominals are *action* nominals, which often occur in the possessive +*-ing* form:

(290) Don's batting is very impressive.
(291) I enjoy her singing.

But (292) below is ambiguous as between a factive and an action nominal – quite a common ambiguity with this structure:

(292) His driving scares me.

'The fact that he drives' versus 'The way he drives'. Some constructions with possessive + *-ing* are clearly factive:

(293) His winning the election pleased few people.
(294) His leaving the country brought disgrace to his family.

Such usages are often called *gerundival*.

The third morphological type, which carries a range of meanings, comprises the 'infinitive' nominals:

(295) To concede defeat would be unwise.
(296) He would like to work.
(297) This book is for me to read.
(298) The book was difficult to understand.

(295) is virtually equivalent to *Conceding defeat now would be unwise*: it is a kind of action nominal. But the infinitive form is often preferred for universal, timeless, statements: *To err is human, To tempt providence would be foolish*, etc. This usage, as the one illustrated in (295), is quite different from those of the infinitives seen in (296)–(298). The embedded sentence in (296) expresses *intention*; that in (297), *use* – both typical functions of the *to*-nominal. (Cf. *This wine is for drinking*.) (298) illustrates another prominent use of the infinitival nominal: attachment to a certain class of 'incomplete' adjectives when they occur in Predicate position:

(299) He was apt to burst out laughing.
(300) She was eager to go.
(301) Mr Brown was willing to take the risk.

Compare this selection of related verbal constructions:

(302) He tended to burst out laughing.
(303) She wanted to go.
(304) Mr Brown agreed to take the risk.
(305) The professor condescended to read his students' essays.
(306) I preferred to go alone.

Though these are all related to the adjectival structures illustrated in (299)–(301), there are some differences among the sentences (302)–(306), as can be seen if we apply what is known as the 'cleft sentence' test to each in turn. (This is a test for the presence of a noun phrase complement.)

(302) (a) *What he tended was to burst out laughing.
(303) (a) What she wanted was to go.
(304) (a) *What Mr Brown agreed was to take the risk.
(305) (a) *What the professor condescended was to read his students' essays.
(306) (a) What I preferred was to go alone.

Apparently, (303) and (306) contain noun phrase complements of the regular kind:

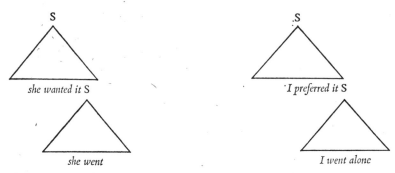

In both sentences there is deletion of *it* and of the repeated *NP* in the constituent, and replacement of the constituent string's *Aux* by *to*. (302), (304), (305) are not derived in that way. Although their embedded constituents are complements, they are not *NP*s, nor parts of *NP*s: they are affixed directly to the *V*s of the matrices, and not to *NP*s; so in the case of (302) we have the structure

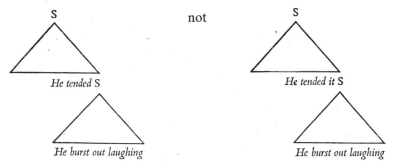

The difference is substantial, as can be seen from (302) (a)–(306) (a): the absence of an *it* marks a construction quite different from the noun phrase complements which have claimed our attention in the

greater part of this chapter. We will say that sentences like (302), (304), (305) contain *verb phrase complements*; (303) and (306), like many other sentences quoted in this chapter, contain noun phrase complements.

Within the limits of this chapter I have been able to give only the most superficial introduction to nominalization, which is a pervasive and productive process linking the deep and surface structures of a large range of sentences. In fact, few sentences fail to display some sign of nominalization. The two chief varieties – complementation and relativization – satisfy the principle of 'parsimony of description' which a grammar tries to obey, for they avoid crippling complexities in the base PSG. An impressive variety of constructions can be referred to a very economical and regular system of transformational rules.

Exercises and topics for discussion

1. Describe the transformational relationships between (279) and (279) (a)–(d) (pp. 131–2 above).
2. Present and analyse some further examples of verb phrase complements.
3. Give a complete derivation, beginning with *S* for each underlying string, for these sentences:

   (a) It annoyed me that the actor forgot his lines.
   (b) I told Stephen to clean himself up.

4. Explain the ambiguity of the following sentences:

   (a) What disturbed John was being disregarded by everyone.
   (b) I disapprove of his playing.
   (c) Moving vehicles can be dangerous.

5. What is the 'cleft sentence test'? Explain its application to (302)–(306) and say exactly what it proves.
6. Discuss in detail the structure of sentences (274)–(276), and design lexical entries for the nominalized verbs they contain.
7. Summarize the arguments for a deep structure element *it* in sentences like (253).

twelve

Relative Clauses and Adjectives Revisited

One of the first examples of transformational structure discussed in this book happened to illustrate relative clauses and adjectives (Ch. 2, examples (24)–(26)). The sentences concerned were used to show how transformations can join simple strings into complex sentences; how they can perform certain modifying operations such as deletion and rearrangement of formatives; and how they explain relationships *between* sentences – in this case, they explain the synonymy of a complex *NP* such as *the black cat* and a simple sentence *the cat was black*. The connections between (24), (25) and (26) are explained by a rather involved set of rules, rules which have implications for structures additional to those in that first series of examples. In this chapter I will discuss relative clauses and some similar, interconnected or contrasted, structures in more detail.

On p. 19 I mentioned a distinction between *restrictive* and *non-restrictive* relative clauses. Now consider another pair of sentences which illustrate this distinction:

(307) Professors who are impressionable give good grades to pretty co-eds.
(308) Professors, who are impressionable, give good grades to pretty co-eds.

These two sentences have quite distinct meanings. (307) asserts that those professors who are impressionable give good grades to pretty co-eds; it implies that there are some professors who are not impressionable, and some professors who don't give good grades to pretty co-eds, but it has no statement to make about these two categories of professor. On the other hand, (308) concerns itself with *all* professors, and makes two assertions about them: that they are impressionable, and that they give good grades to pretty co-eds. According to (308), there are no professors without these two (perhaps unrelated) qualities.

Of course, the distinction which we are now considering does not have to do exclusively with the *all/some* contrast, as can be realized from the following pair:

(309) The student who was sitting in the library fell asleep.
(310) The student, who was sitting in the library, fell asleep.

Just as the embedded sentence in (307) restricts the reference of *professors* (some professors, i.e. those who are impressionable), so the one in (309) delimits the reference of the *NP the student*: the student is *identified* as the one who was sitting in the library, and the embedded clause performs a defining function. On the other hand, the subordinate clause in (310) does not define the Subject-*NP*, but simply attaches a non-defining Predicate to it. It would seem that the embedded strings of (307), (309) have a 'restricting', 'defining', 'specifying' or 'identifying' function which is not a property of the embedded constituents in (308), (310): let us call them *restrictive* relative clauses; the embedded constituents of (308), (310) are *non-restrictive*, or, better, *appositive*. Appositive strings are not considered to be relative clauses: despite the superficial similarity, they are a quite different kind of thing. So we may simply distinguish between relative and appositive clauses.

What is the distinctive characteristic of relative clauses in deep structure? It appears that a relative clause modifies the meaning of the *N* to which it relates very much as *Det* does: cf. *some professors/ professors who are impressionable*. In particular, the relative clause function seems to have some connection with the Universality/ Definiteness/Proximateness/Quantification features which are developed under *Det* in deep structure (see Ch. 6, pp. 64–7). By this I mean that a relative clause limits the generality of reference of an *N* in much the same way as do features like [Quant], [±Prox], etc.; compare the pairs

(311) That boy . . .
(312) The boy who is sitting over there . . .
(313) Sóme boys . . .
(314) Boys who run away from school . . .

Of course there is a big difference between quantitative restriction and relative clause restriction, since the relative clause assigns specific lexical information to the *N*, whereas [Quant], say, does not. Nevertheless, I am suggesting that, say, *professors who are impressionable* (equivalently, *impressionable professors*) stands in somewhat the same relation to *professors* as does *sóme professors*: *professors* lacks a restrictive feature which is present in the other forms – in *sóme professors* it is [Quant], in *impressionable professors* it is a set of semantic features analogous in function to the syntactic feature [Quant]. These features must, in turn, be accommodated by some syntactic feature in deep structure; just what this feature is, it is impossible to say at the moment, but it seems certain that relative clauses (and associated prenominal adjectives) are permitted only when such a feature, which we might call [+ R], is selected while *Det* is being developed. The relation of [+ R] to other features in the *Det* system is a question for further research. At least we can assume that appositive clauses do not depend on [+ R]. It is presence of [+ R], then, which probably distinguishes (307) and (309) from (308) and (310) in deep structure. Without some device like [+ R] it would be necessary to say that, for instance, (307) and (308) had the same deep structure –

Professors give good grades to pretty co-eds
Professors are impressionable

– and we would lack an explanation for the fact that (307) and (308) have different meanings, since by definition different transformations cannot produce different meanings.

However, convincing circumstantial evidence for the contrast between relative and appositive clauses comes from the different transformational connections which each type has with other sentences. (315) is more convincingly a paraphrase of (307) than of (308):

(315)   Impressionable professors give good grades to pretty co-eds.

On the other hand, (316) is a paraphrase of (308) but not of (307):

(316)   Professors give good grades to pretty co-eds and are impressionable.

Similarly, (317) is a paraphrase of (309) but not of (310), while (318) and (319) paraphrase (310) but not (309):

(317)   The student sitting in the library fell asleep.
(318)   The student fell asleep sitting in the library.
(319)   The student was sitting in the library and fell asleep.

In all cases of apposition – in effect, (308), (310), (316), (319) amongst the present examples – the sentence consists of two separate strings making two separate statements about the same topic; in all cases of restrictive embedding – (307), (309), (315), (317) – the constituent string serves to 'specify' an *N* in the matrix string, so that the complex sentence as a whole makes only one overall statement. (Apposition resembles conjoining more than it does relativization; one might even say that conjoining is a form of apposition.)

Let us now concentrate on relative clauses proper – embedded strings attached to an *NP* in the matrix where the *Det* of that *NP* contains the feature [+ R].

In order for relativization to occur, we must have two underlying strings which have at least one *NP* in common (syntactically equivalent and co-referential) and of the repeated *NP*s one must be marked [+ R]; thus:

> The student [+ R] was sitting in the library.
> The student fell asleep.

If both of the *NP*s were marked [+ R], then either could be the matrix. One possibility is shown in (309); the other is

(320)   The student who fell asleep was sitting in the library.

But it is clear that only one string may contain a repeated *NP* marked [+ R]; otherwise there would be no way of showing the difference between (309) and (320), yet these sentences have different meanings.

If the repeated *NP* is the Subject of the matrix, it may equally well be either the Subject or the Object of the constituent, and if it is the Object of the matrix, again it is immaterial whether it occurs in Subject or Object function in the constituent. The range of possibilities is reflected in the following sentences:

(309)   The student who was sitting in the library fell asleep.
(321)   I saw the student who was sitting in the library.
(322)   (= 280) The idea that he presented surprised us.
(323)   He announced the discovery that he had made.

Relativization where the constituent sentence is of the type encountered in (322) and (323) – Object relativized – is only one step more complicated than it is in the case of (309) and (321) – Subject relativized. In both cases, the first step is to insert the constituent string immediately to the right of the matched *NP* of the matrix; the matrix will be identified by the presence of a feature [+ R] in the *Det* of the appropriate *NP*, of course:

> The student – the student was sitting in the library – fell asleep.
> The idea – he presented the idea – surprised us.

(Note that in a proper derivation these strings would be represented as sequenced sets of features; I write them as orthographic sentences for the sake of readability.) In the case of (322), an extra move is necessary to relocate the relativized *NP* in direct juxtaposition with its twin in the matrix:

The idea – the idea he presented – surprised us.

(The same step is necessary if the constituent string is passive and the relativized *NP* is the agent:

(324)   The man – the silver was stolen by the man – ran away into the darkness.
The man – the man the silver was stolen by – ran away into the darkness.)

Next, the *Det* of the relativized *NP* is replaced by a *wh*-pronoun form, by a feature-transfer rule of a kind which should by now be quite familiar, and I show its effect in shorthand form:

The student – *wh*-student was sitting in the library – fell asleep.
The idea – *wh*-idea he presented – surprised us.

In modern English, the *N* of the relativized *NP* is deleted:

The student – *wh*- was sitting in the library – fell asleep.
The idea – *wh*- he presented – surprised us.

I say 'in modern English' because deletion of the repeated *N* was not obligatory in the English of the Renaissance or even somewhat later – this tolerance of the repeated *N* in an earlier stage of our language might be thought to lend some support to the intermediate stage of the present analysis, in which it was decided to retain the *N* and prepose *wh*- rather than to replace *N* by *wh*- in one single step.

Finally, the symbol *wh*- is realized as an appropriate form *who(m)/ that* or *which/that*, and the string boundaries – . . . – are removed to integrate the relative clause phonologically in its matrix. Note that the realization rule must take account of the fact that, if the relativized *NP* contains the feature [+ Human] (e.g. *professor, student*), *wh*- must be rendered as *who* or *that* if it is the Subject of the constituent, and *who* or (conservatively) *whom*, or *that*, if it is the Object; but that if the relativized *NP* contains [– Human] (e.g. *idea, water, camel*) it must appear as *which* or *that*, regardless of whether it is Subject or Object in the constituent. The details of the rules which transfer these features from *N* to *Det* and thus to *wh*- are too intricate to present in the space available here, but their general design falls within the type of rule illustrated when I discussed *NP*s and pronouns in Chs. 6 and 9.

Once relative clause embedding has taken place, various modifications become available. The chief of these is *relative pronoun deletion*, which is permissible in some constructions but not in others:

(325) The idea [*which*] he presented surprised us.
(326) The girl [*who was*] sitting on the beach remained quite impassive.
(327) The boy [*who was*] noticed by the talent scout was an extremely gifted player.

But not

(328) *The man [*who had*] stolen the silver ran away into the darkness.
(329) *The girl [*who was*] impassive sat on the beach.
(330) *Bankers [*who are*] capitalists lack popularity.
(331) *Professors [*who are*] impressionable give good grades to pretty co-eds.
(332) *Professors [*who*] give good grades to pretty co-eds are impressionable.

(325) shows that *wh-* may be deleted where the relativized *NP* is the Object of the constituent string; (326) that *wh-* and *be* may disappear if the constituent's *Aux* contains [+Prog]; (327) that this same deletion may take place if the constituent string is Passive. On the other hand, deletion must not take place if the constituent is marked Perfect Aspect (see (328)) or Momentary or Habitual Aspect ((329)–(332)). However, (332) differs from (329)–(331), since the rearranged structures (333)–(335) are permissible, but not (336):

(333) The impassive girl sat on the beach.
(334) Capitalist bankers lack popularity.
(335) Impressionable professors give good grades to pretty co-eds.
(336) *Give good grades to pretty co-eds professors are impressionable.

The facts of the situation seem to be that relative pronoun deletion may after all apply to the strings underlying (329)–(331) – but not (328), (332) – but *only* if a subsequent rearranging transformation is applied. This is, of course, the *adjective-preposing* transformation, which was first applied as long ago as example (24). We now see that it is responsible for 'adjectivalizing' certain predicative *NP*s as well as for preposing predicative adjectives: see sentence (334). What is most important about this analysis is that it derives prenominal adjectives and nouns by subjecting strings in which they are predicates to the relativization process. It is intuitively obvious that prenominal adjectives and nouns, as in (333)–(335), are *restrictive* in the technical sense offered by this chapter; the present analysis, by making them dependent on relativization, provides a natural explanation for this intuition.

(As a final note on the prenominal positioning of adjectives, observe that the process just described is permissible only when the predicative adjective is *final* in the constituent string. Where the adjective is followed by a prepositional phrase (337), relative pronoun deletion can take place (338), but prenominal repositioning is barred (339):

(337) The craftsman who was expert at diamond-cutting passed on the art to his son.
(338) The craftsman expert at diamond-cutting passed on the art to his son.
(339) *The expert at diamond-cutting craftsman passed on the art to his son.

A parallel constraint prevents prenominal repositioning in the case of constructions like (326), (327).)

We now return to *appositive* constructions. As we have seen, these enjoy surface structures which approximate closely to those of relatives:

(309) The student who was sitting in the library fell asleep.
(310) The student, who was sitting in the library, fell asleep.

Appositives are like relatives in their word-order and their utilization of a *wh*-form; they are also amenable to deletion of the relative pronoun and of *be*:

(340) The student, sitting in the library, fell asleep.

Other superficial similarities to restrictive structures will be noticed shortly. Before we draw attention to similarity in surface structure, however, we must provide a way of accounting for the underlying difference between these two types of construction. The difference can be attributed formally to presence or absence of $[+R]$ in the underlying representation for one *NP* in the matrix. Additionally, we must show that appositives are basically like conjoined structures. For a start, one can propose that the following four sentences have the same deep structure (an interpretation which was implied in the notion of 'paraphrase' on p. 141 above):

(308) Professors, who are impressionable, give good grades to · pretty co-eds.
(316) Professors give good grades to pretty co-eds and are impressionable.

145

(341) Professors, who give good grades to pretty co-eds, are impressionable.

(342) Professors are impressionable and give good grades to pretty co-eds.

We may show the difference between (308) and (341) and their relativized counterparts by making their derivations pass through a conjoining operation. Whereas, for (307) (p. 139 above), the constituent *professors are impressionable* is attached to the [+R] *NP* of the matrix, the same string is first conjoined to the right of the other string in the case of (308) and (316):

(307) Professors – professors are impressionable – give good grades to pretty co-eds.

(308) Professors give good grades to pretty co-eds – and professors are impressionable.

Given the latter string, a choice of further processes is available. By deletion of the repeated *NP*, a normal conjoined construction (316) is obtained. Alternatively, the whole of the right-hand string, including the conjunction *and*, may be placed to the right of *professors* in the left-hand string:

Professors – and professors are impressionable – give good grades to pretty co-eds.

This is the direct basis for apposition. The retention of *and* in the above complex string is most important. Ultimately, it serves as a cue for the insertion of the commas (as in (308)); in the intermediate stages of the derivation it distinguishes appositive strings from relatives, so that, even though several modifications typical of relatives are permitted – e.g. *wh-* and *Aux*-deletion as in (340) – a restrictive clause cannot be derived.

A final observation on relatives and appositives is that appositives may be hidden in *any* relative-type surface structure. If the constituent is embedded as above, it is subject to all the formal operations of relativization, provided that *and* is preserved to block the restrictive function. However, in the final stages *and* may disappear from surface structure, so we have some structures which are ambiguous as between restrictive and appositive. Of (333)–(335) above I said that prenominal adjectives and nouns are *restrictive*. It would be nearer the truth to say that prenominal adjectives and nouns are ambiguous as far as the restrictive/appositive distinction is concerned, although in the majority of cases a restrictive interpretation is more natural. Reconsidering (334), we find that it has two alternative interpretations:

(334)   Capitalist bankers lack popularity.

This may mean either (a) 'those bankers who are capitalists lack popularity' or (b) 'bankers lack popularity and are capitalists'. Arguably, to be a banker is also to be a capitalist, and so the pre-posed *capitalist* in (334) *cannot* be restrictive – all the features of *capitalist* are already present in *banker*, so *capitalist* cannot further specify the meaning of *banker*; hence the interpretation (b). How-ever, if one does not believe that all bankers are capitalists, then interpretation (a) is possible. With the (b) reading, compare

(343)   Long-necked giraffes pluck their food from the trees.

which does not provoke the question 'Where do *short-necked* giraffes get their food?' Again, in (344) below, *ferocious* seems to be appositive, while *hungry* in (345) is more likely to be restrictive:

(344)   Ferocious lions are dangerous.

('Lions are dangerous and lions are ferocious.')

(345)   Hungry lions are dangerous.

('Those lions who are hungry are dangerous' – not 'Lions are danger-ous and lions are hungry'.)

It seems that a preposed adjective or *NP* is likely to be understood as appositive if it is semantically quasi-redundant. If all bankers are capitalists, all giraffes have long necks and all lions are ferocious, one cannot attribute these qualities to them restrictively, because no additional, defining information is supplied. However, since lions are not always hungry, (345) must imply restriction. The difference between (334), (343) and (344) on the one hand, and (345) on the other, exactly parallels that between (308) and (307)/(315) or (310) and (309)/(317):

[+R]	[−R]
Professors who arc impressionable give good grades to pretty co-eds.	Professors, who are impressionable, give good grades to pretty co-eds.
The boy who was sitting in the library fell asleep.	The boy, who was sitting in the library, fell asleep.
The boy sitting in the library fell asleep.	The boy was sitting in the library and fell asleep.
Capitalist bankers lack popularity (a).	Capitalist bankers lack popularity (b).
Hungry lions are dangerous.	Ferocious lions are dangerous.
	Long-necked giraffes pluck their food from the trees.

(344) and (345), in which the contrast between *ferocious* and *hungry* in some way determines whether the preposed adjective is appositive or restrictive, make it obvious that we are dealing with very delicate

semantic questions here. A further example drives the point home. Although (343) raises no question about short-necked giraffes, possibly (346) does:

(346)   Long-necked giraffes pluck their food from *the top of* trees.

Is it implied that short-necked giraffes browse off the lower branches? If *long-necked* is appositive in (343) but restrictive in (346), how exactly does the word *top*, tucked away in a distant corner of the constituent structure, make all the difference? This is obviously an extremely intricate problem in syntactic/semantic relationships, one which TG in its present state of development is not properly equipped to handle. But it has enabled us to formulate the problem fairly exactly. At least, our discussion of relatives and appositives has delineated areas for further research within a transformational framework. It has also underlined a point made in Ch. 2: that sentences are not all they seem on the surface; even (315), it now appears, is ambiguous:

(315)   Impressionable professors give good grades to pretty co-eds.

Exercises and topics for discussion

1. Define as precisely as you can the notions 'restrictive' and 'appositive'. To what extent do these relationships depend on *semantic* restrictions between nouns and adjectives?
2. Suggest, informally, how the feature [+ R] might be incorporated in a modified analysis of *Det*.
3. Illustrate relativization of Objects in a selection of examples of your own choice.
4. State in detail the restrictions on selection of *who, whom, which* and *that*.
5. Add some other relevant sentences to the list (325)–(332) and work out the situations in which relative pronoun deletion may take place (a) without and (b) with subsequent adjective-preposing.
6. What irregularities do you detect in the following sentences?
    (a) *The sitting in the library student fell asleep.
    (b) *The eaten by the gorilla banana was unripe.
    (c) *The person about I told you has died.
    (d) *The thin as a rake prisoner had been ill-treated.
7. Extend the rules for appositives mentioned in this chapter so that they cater for the following structures:
    (a) Sitting in the library, the student fell asleep.
    (b) Having eaten his lunch, he took a nap.

(c) Short, dapper, balding Lou Stankowicz, 38, has already established a big reputation as manager of the Los Angeles team.

(d) Mr Stankowicz, nervous and tense but apparently optimistic, explained his plans for the team's future.

8. Provide a general definition of the concept of nominalization.
9. Define the following terms:
   (a) node
   (b) initial symbol
   (c) discontinuous constituent
   (d) agreement
   (e) aspect
   (f) transformation
   (g) object
   (h) right-branching
   (i) structural description
   (j) generate

thirteen

Conjoining Transformations

In Ch. 10 a distinction was drawn between two types of complex sentence: the type generated by *embedding* transformations and the type generated by *conjoining* transformations. The difference between the two varieties can be diagrammed thus:

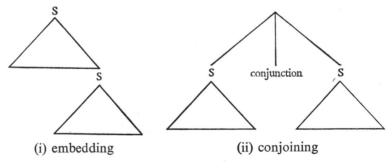

(i) embedding   (ii) conjoining

In (i) we see that one underlying P-marker dominates another – the matrix-constituent relationship: this is 'domination' in the technical sense of the term in syntax; one S node dominates another S node. But in (ii) there is no domination: neither S node is higher in the tree than the other, and the top node of the tree is unlabelled, for the branching below it does not define an S, but a conjunction of Ss. The syntactic notion of domination reflects, rather loosely, the intuition we may have that one part of a complex sentence may be more important than the other(s), or alternatively that the separate parts may be of equal status. I say 'rather loosely' because some conjoined structures display a kind of logical dependency between the parts which suggests priority of one part over another:

150

(347) John slammed the door and walked into the garden.

Contrast:

(348) John opened the door and Peter opened the window.

The priority of the first clause in (347) over the second should not hide the fact that its syntactic analysis is the same as that of (348), at least by comparison with embedding constructions – neither sentence exhibits domination.

Conjoining is a process by which two or more underlying strings are joined together, without domination, to make a complex sentence or part of a complex sentence. Thus, (349) and (350) are conjoined to form (351); (352) and (353) to make (354):

(349) John likes swimming.
(350) Peter prefers to sail.
(351) John likes swimming but Peter prefers to sail.

(352) My aunt is an expert at karate.
(353) My uncle has learnt to defend himself.
(354) My aunt is an expert at karate and my uncle has learnt to defend himself.

Since an indefinite number of strings may be conjoined in this way, conjunction is one of the devices which ensure that there is no longest sentence in a natural language. The following sequence, for instance, may always be made one constituent longer by reapplication of the conjoining transformation to the complex sentence and one additional string:

(355) My aunt is an expert at karate and my uncle has learnt to defend himself and their children have all practised judo from infancy and the dog is a trained guard dog and they are all very friendly to visitors . . .

One optional modification to such structures is that any particular sequence three or more constituents long may have every *and* but the last one deleted and replaced by a comma:

(356) My aunt is an expert at karate, my uncle has learnt to defend himself, their children have all practised judo from infancy, the dog is a trained guard dog (,) and they are all very friendly to visitors.

The comma before the final, obligatory, *and* is optional.

Such examples as the above suggest that conjoining is an extremely simple process – just a matter of putting an *and*, *or*, *but* or comma between the end of one constituent and the beginning of the next.

However, if you look at the specialized literature on the subject, you will see that conjoining is a highly involved part of linguistic structure, some aspects of which have not yet been adequately explained. Certainly, a full account of conjoining, reflecting the many detailed restrictions on which constituents may be conjoined and how, would need much more than a few general rules. Here I will simply report some of the better established facts, and better defined problems, about conjoining, making no attempt to capture the truth of the situation in formal rules.

First, two preparatory remarks about certain restrictions on conjoining. There are constraints on what kinds of strings can be conjoined, and on what conjunctions can be used between certain strings. If two strings have been subjected to transformational modification (e.g. nominalization), their transformational histories must be similar if they are to be conjoined. This condition explains why (357) is grammatical, (358)–(362) not:

(357)   Eating and drinking can be overdone.
(358)   *Eating and to drink can be overdone.
(359)   *I like to eat and what my wife cooks.
(360)   *Punctuality and to know what time to leave impress me.
(361)   *Why have you come here and go away.
(362)   *Shut the door and last time you slammed it.

As well as the clearly ungrammatical linkings of such sentences as these, there are also semantically odd, 'pointless' combinations:

(363)   This is a Picasso and my daughter likes strawberries.
(364)   Cabbages are green and I read quite a lot.

It is difficult to know with certainty whether a grammar should be responsible for preventing the generation of such conjoinings. At the moment, we do not possess a semantic description which could handle facts of usage such as these, so we cannot investigate their representation within grammar. They are, however, quite probably outside the scope of linguistic description.

The other restriction concerns the permissibility of particular conjunctions in relation to particular pairings of strings. Conjunctions are not interchangeable, and which one may be selected depends on the strings being conjoined:

(365)   John and Alison are coming.
(366)   John or Alison is coming.
(367)   *John but Alison is coming.
(368)   John and not Alison is coming.
(369)   John but not Alison is coming.

(370)   *John or not Alison is coming.
(351)   John likes swimming but Peter prefers to sail.
(371)   John likes swimming and Peter prefers to sail.
(372)   *John likes swimming or Peter prefers to sail.
(373)   *He closed the window but closed the door.

and so on. No one has, to my knowledge, worked out the exact distributional privileges of these conjunctions; again, in order to do so one would have to possess a very delicate mechanism of semantic analysis.

Of the many examples of conjoined sentences so far given in this chapter, only three have surface structures which approximate at all closely to the situation diagrammed as (ii) on p. 150 above – two full underlying strings articulated one after the other with a conjunction in between:

(348)   John opened the door and Peter opened the window.
(351)   John likes swimming but Peter prefers to sail.
(354)   My aunt is an expert at karate and my uncle has learnt to defend himself.

Other examples involve some reduction in the length of the string and consequent change of structure. Presumably, (347) for instance is, beneath the surface, a complex sentence of type (ii):

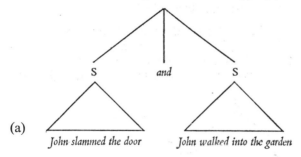

(a)

But the omission of the second *John* dramatically alters the superficial constituent structure (here simplified):

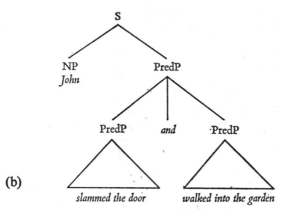

(b)

Notice that the transformation which changes the P-marker (a) into
(b) is *obligatory*: if an identical *NP* occurs in both of two conjoined
strings, one must be deleted; sentence (374) below is ungrammatical
unless *John ≠ John*:

(374)   *John slammed the door and John walked into the garden.

The same consideration applies to the derivations of (316), (319) and
(342) in Ch. 12. A simpler example than these is the following:

(375)   He has persevered and triumphed.

which is presumably based on the pair *He has persevered/He has
triumphed*. This example shows how thoroughly the conjoined
sentences are intermingled on the deletion of the repeated *NP*: they
are linked in such a way that *Aux* is shared by both of the *V*s:

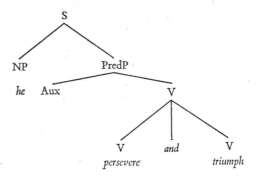

We might say that here a conjunction of sentences is disguised as a
conjunction of *V*s. A similar analysis applies to sentences containing
repeated *NP*s when the varied *PredP* is *Aux + Adj* –

154

(376)   Camels are irritable and untrustworthy.

or *Aux + NP* –

(377)   My grandfather was a scholar and a poet.

An analogous situation is found in sentences where the conjoined strings are identical down to, but not including, the Object-*NP*:

(378)   He writes articles and stories.

This has the analysis

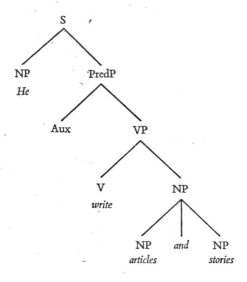

Compare (379), in which each conjoined string is nominalized:

(379)   We like visiting Scotland and Ireland.

All my remarks so far have concerned changes in constituent structure governed by repetition of the Subject-*NP* in two conjoined strings. Where it is part of the *PredP* which is held constant in the two strings, the rules allow more latitude. Where the whole of the *PredP* is repeated, surface structure is a sort of 'mirror-image' of the arrangement diagrammed above for conjoined sentences with repeated Subjects; recursive branching is found on the left rather than the right of the tree:

155

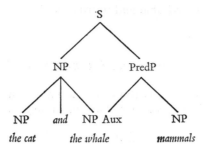

(380)   The cat and the whale are [both] mammals.

Where the repeated element is *V*, one occurrence may be deleted, or it may be retained:

(348)   John opened the door and Peter opened the window.
(381)   John opened the door and Peter the window.

Similarly, a repeated Object-*NP* may either be pronominalized or deleted:

(382)   John unlocked and opened the door.
(383)   John unlocked the door and opened it.
(384)   John unlocked and Peter opened the door.
(385)   John unlocked the door and Peter opened it.

Finally, there is a kind of 'criss-cross' conjoining structure which may be used whether or not any elements are repeated (and deleted):

(386)   John and Peter [respectively] unlocked and opened the door and the window.
(387)   John and Peter opened and closed the window and the door, respectively.

'Respectively' indicates that the words are criss-crossed in this way:

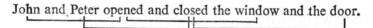

Awkward as this particular construction is, simpler versions are acceptable and usual:

(388)   Mary and June knit and sew.

(where, for the purposes of this discussion, it is not implied that both of them knit and sew). I mention this structure only because it may be relevant to the question: how do P-markers like (a) turn into

P-markers like (b)? (see pp. 153–4 above). It is not obvious that repeated *NP*s are deleted *in situ*, as it were:

John slammed the door and [~~John~~] walked into the garden.

Such mechanical deletion would not explain the *structural* change between (a) and (b): that is, it would not show how the left-most *NP* becomes Subject of the right-most *PredP*. The existence of the 'respectively' construction, as in (388), suggests the possibility of a useful intermediate string which helps explain this structural fact. Suppose we want to derive

(389)   Mary knits and sews.

What has to be shown is that *Mary* is the Subject of *sews*. From the string

Mary knits and Mary' sews

(in which *Mary* = *Mary'*) we derive an intermediate 'criss-cross' string parallel to the one actually underlying (388):

Mary and Mary' knits and sews.

In effect, a P-marker intermediate between the (a)-type and the (b)-type has been provided, in which the repeated *NP*s have been conjoined, and the non-repeated *V*s:

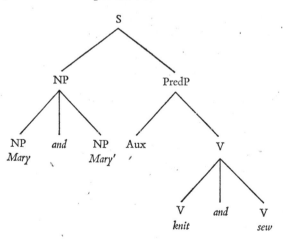

Next, *and Mary'* is deleted. The importance of this intermediate P-marker before deletion is that it provides a way of associating *sew* with *Mary* before *Mary'* is deleted: it identifies the Subject of *sew*. It is possible that manœuvres such as this are necessary to explain the origin of the other types of 'reduced' sentences mentioned in the last few pages, but the exact operation of this intermediate stage in conjoining in a range of constructions has still to be investigated.

We now turn to an aspect of conjoining which has preoccupied linguists in recent years. Compare the following two sentences:

(390)   I found a necklace and a bracelet.
(391)   I like peaches and cream.

(390) can be derived confidently from two constituent strings which, if realized as separate sentences, would be *I found a necklace* and *I found a bracelet*. But does not the suggestion of a parallel deep structure for (391) fail to do justice to its meaning? A deep structure *I like peaches/I like cream* implies that there is no particular connection between the speaker's fondness for peaches and his fondness for cream; but surely he is saying that he is fond of the combination 'peaches and cream'. On this reading, there is a considerable difference between the surface Object-*NP*s of (390) and (391): it would seem that, while (390), like all the other examples given so far, is a conjunction of sentences, (391) is a conjunction but not a conjunction of sentences. In addition to the difference of lexical items, (390) and (391) have different deep syntaxes. This difference appears to be consistent for a whole range of complex sentences each of which has two alternative underlying structures; in the examples below, each of the paraphrases (a) bases the sentence concerned on two underlying sentences conjoined regularly, whereas (b) suggests a second reading *not* based on sentence-like strings:

(392)   Sticks and stones may break my bones.
    (a) Sticks may break my bones and stones may break my bones.
    (b) The combination of sticks and stones may break my bones.

(393)   Peter and Jane are married.
    (a) Peter is a married man and Jane is a married woman.
    (b) They are married to each other.

(394)   Professor Smith and Professor Jones write college textbooks.
    (a) Both of these professors are writers of academic texts.
    (b) The two of them together are co-authors of texts.

Now consider some unambiguous sentences which can receive a (b)-type interpretation but not an (a)-type:

(395)   The car and the truck collided.
    (Not based on *The car collided and the truck collided.*)

(396) Two and two are four.
(Not based on *Two is four and two is four.*)

(397) Oil and water don't mix.
(Not based on *Oil doesn't mix and water doesn't mix.*)

(398) Candidate A and Candidate B are similar in their political beliefs.
(Not based on *Candidate A is similar in his political beliefs and candidate B is similar in his political beliefs.*)

(399) Peter and John are in agreement with each other.
(Not based on *Peter is in agreement and John is in agreement.*)

Notice that most sentences of this type have alternative versions with *to, with,* or *from* (whichever is appropriate), and that the resulting structures are reversible:

(400) Peter is married to Jane/Jane is married to Peter.
(401) The truck collided with the car/The car collided with the truck.
(402) Oil doesn't mix with water/Water doesn't mix with oil.

and so on. These transformations do not apply to complex sentences founded on a regular conjunction of full, sentence-like strings:

(403) (cf. (380))   *The whale is a mammal with the cat.

Such evidence as the above suggests that there are (at least) two kinds of conjoining process, represented by examples (390) and (391). (390) has an intermediate structure approximately as follows:

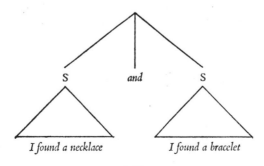

159

(391), on the other hand, appears to have a quite different structure:

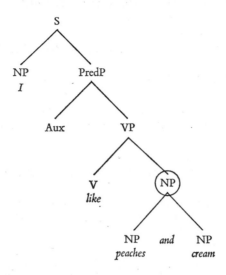

The circled *NP* node in this tree-diagram establishes *peaches and cream* as a single constituent in deep structure, unlike *a necklace and a bracelet*, which is clearly shown to be derived from the combination of two *NPs* originating from separate deep structure strings. Contemporary linguists recognize this distinction by calling (390) an example of *sentence conjunction* and (391) (likewise (392) (b), (393) (b), (394) (b), (395)–(399)) an instance of *phrasal conjunction*. This way of differentiating the two types seems to accord well with one's intuition of the basic structural distinction, but the problem must be faced that such a distinction is very difficult to formalize in terms of the resources of our particular version of deep structure. Phrasal conjunction demands radical modification of our design for the base syntax.

In an attempt to define the problem – we cannot dream of solving it at the moment – let us consider one final example. Sentence (404) is ambiguous as between sentence conjunction and phrase conjunction origins for its compound Subject-*NP*:

(404)   Mary and Jane play the piano well.

This means either (a) 'Mary and Jane are accomplished piano duettists' or (b) 'Mary plays the piano well and Jane plays the piano well' with no reference to their playing duets together. In both cases, the following partial phrase-marker appears in the derivation:

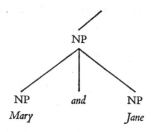

With this part of the P-marker for interpretation (a), compare the bottom right section of the P-marker for (391) above; and with interpretation (b) compare the P-marker for (389) – or for (388) if we substitute *June* for *Mary'* – given on p. 157 above. This configuration is structurally identical for (a) and (b), but its status differs from one to the other. In (b) this is part of a *derived* P-marker based on an earlier P-marker

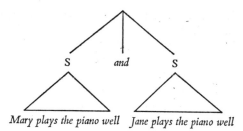

Mary plays the piano well   *Jane plays the piano well*

In (a), however, the sub-construction *Mary and Jane* must be one phrase in the deep structure, since it serves as a semantic whole— 'Mary and Jane together'.

The trouble is that if *Mary and Jane* in (404) (a) has its origin in deep structure, we need a branching rule of a kind which has been carefully excluded from the present model of syntax:

*NP→NP + conjunction + NP

This is evidently a recursive rule: the same symbol occurs on the left and the right of the arrow, and so the output of the rule can serve as its input in an unlimited number of reapplications. In Ch. 10, pp. 117–19, I argued that recursive rules are unacceptable in the base PSG. In view of the reality of phrasal conjunction, we must either abandon this restriction or find some other explanation for structures such as (404) (a). In any event, some modification or enrichment of the base PSG is evidently necessary. Many possibilities, some more radical than others, are available. One suggestion that has been made is that the Number system of *Det* might be modified, so that *Mary and Jane* in (404) (b) could be marked 'plural', *Mary and Jane* in (404) (a) something like 'dual' or 'combined'. So the deep structure of (404) (a) and other instances of phrasal conjunction might contain the sub-string

$$\begin{bmatrix} +\text{Comb} \\ . \\ . \\ . \\ +F_n \end{bmatrix} + \begin{bmatrix} +\text{N} \\ . \\ . \\ . \\ +F_n \end{bmatrix}$$

and the feature [+Comb] under *Det* might trigger an obligatory transformation duplicating the feature-set for *N* to produce

$$[+\text{Comb}] + [+\text{N}] + [+\text{N}]$$

In this way we would avoid the anomalous rewriting rule by shifting the recursive function to the transformational component of the grammar.

This hypothetical solution to the problem raised by phrasal conjunction has not been fully worked out and may come to nothing. I end the descriptive part of this book with the problem and a tentative solution, hoping thereby to dramatize the fact that transformational grammar is not a closed discipline, but is still undergoing modification; and that its present uncertainties promise well for continuing vitality in the future.

Exercises and topics for discussion

1. Define carefully the distinction between *embedded* and *conjoined* constructions.
2. What is a recursive rule? Illustrate as many types of complex sentences with recursive properties as you can.
3. Provide an extensive classified list of grammatical and ungrammatical sentences designed to show the distributional differences between the conjunctions *and, or* and *but*.
4. Discuss and illustrate deletion and pronominalization of repeated *NP*s in embedding and conjoining transformations, comparing the treatment of repeated Subjects and repeated Objects in conjoining.
5. Identify and discuss the ambiguity of the following sentences:
   (a) John and Mary dance.
   (b) They amuse themselves.
   (c) The students bought the new book.
   (d) John and Mary were carrying baskets.
   (e) The busker played a trumpet and a drum.
   (f) John sang and danced.

6. In the light of sentences 5. (a)–(f), redefine the notion of phrasal conjunction.

7. Explore further the implications of the 'criss-cross' structure in accounting for deletion in conjoining.

8. Provide some pairs of sentences which bring out the relationship between apposition and sentence conjunction.

fourteen

Postscript: Linguistic Universals and the Nature of Grammatical Descriptions

In the nineteenth century, virtually the whole effort of descriptive linguistics was concentrated on quite a small selection of the languages of the world. Linguists worked almost exclusively on members of the Indo-European 'family' of languages: Latin, Greek, Sanskrit, English, German, French, the Scandinavian languages, Russian and the other Slavonic tongues, and so on. These languages, although superficially very different, have underlying similarities attributable to the fact that they are historically related: they are all offshoots, diversified through time and through the rise and fall of populations, of one primitive ancestor in pre-history. The comparative method of nineteenth-century historical philology brought out many similarities, some trivial and some profound, between the languages studied. We could say that this study produced implicit agreement on a common grammatical framework – which was not transformational, nor properly generative, of course. A grammar written for one language can be expected to have characteristics which are transferable to another language if that other language is historically related. And the comparative technique naturally emphasized and reinforced these transferable qualities.

Around the turn of the century, the attention of linguists was directed to a much wider range of languages, including many which have no historical connection with the Indo-European tongues. In particular, American anthropologists became interested in the languages of the indigenous peoples of their continent, partly because learning these languages was essential to a real understanding of American Indian cultures, and partly because it was realized that the cultures, and the languages too, were under threat from advancing 'civilization': thus they had to be recorded in writing before they became extinct. At this point in the argument, a practical difficulty presented itself: the categories of linguistic analysis which had been developed for Indo-European reflected, rather stiffly and exclusively, the characteristics of Indo-European languages, and so the available mode of analysis turned out to be less than suitable for these newly discovered non-Indo-European tongues. As more and more 'exotic' languages were investigated in detail, linguists were confronted with an unmanageable diversity of types of structure quite alien to the Indo-European mould. The suspicion grew up – and it was soon stated outright – that languages could differ from each other in an infinite number of ways: that, moving from one language to another, one had absolutely no way of predicting what the grammar of the second language would be like.

American structural linguists stressed the methodological implications of this proposition. As far as the practical analysis of languages was concerned, they made it a cardinal tenet that 'each language must be described *in its own terms*'. In general, this meant that analytic techniques had to be devised which were language-unspecific, flexible enough to apply to any language, whatever its structural peculiarities. In particular, the assertion meant that one's description of one language must not be influenced by prejudices stemming from other languages one knew or had studied.

The methodological bias of American structural linguistics in the period to about 1955 obscured the fact that these injunctions about the flexibility of analytic technique implied a quite audacious theoretical assertion: *that there are no restrictions on the forms which human languages may assume.*

Now it is certainly true that human languages display impressive structural differences one from another. The distribution of populations being what it is, one would expect wide structural differences. But one would not expect these differences to be entirely without restriction. Human language appears to be a communication system of a determinate design. We know that human language is formally distinct from, say, bee-dancing, the courtship rituals of birds and fish, the vocal responses of apes, symbolic logic, musical conventions, gesture, and the many other communication systems which exist in the observable world of animal behaviour. The design-features of language differ, in describable ways, from the design-features of other known devices used in animal communication. What I am

165

saying is that there *are* design-features, formal qualities which are shared by all languages and not enjoyed by phenomena which are not language. On biological grounds alone, we must predict some constancy of design common to all languages. Language is a 'natural' phenomenon, in that the human organism seems to be, uniquely, innately disposed to learn language; other organisms do not, and in the species which have been tested, cannot, learn language. This being so, one must argue a specific biological propensity to language (contrast chess, symbolic logic, etc., which are not acquired by the majority of people). To take the argument one stage further, if language is biologically universal, it is likely that its design is universal, since the physiology and morphology of human beings do not differ importantly within the species. The structure of the central nervous system must determine, in some as yet unknown way, the disposition to acquire and use language; and since there are not significant differences in the central nervous system from one individual human being to another, we would expect this biological constant to determine *formal* constants in language. In specific terms, we assume that biological uniformity ensures that some general features (e.g. the use of transformations) occur in all languages, and beyond this that it limits the range of variable features: defines the limits within which variations attributable to the environment of speakers may range (e.g. that there should be no transformations of a certain type).

These assumptions have immediate implications for language-learning and for grammar-writing. I shall deal with language-learning very briefly, although this is a fiercely controversial topic. It seems safe to assume that all normal children are born with a specific disposition to learn language; but that they will not learn language except when their environment provides the example of linguistic usage, and the motivation of communicative need, to set the language-learning process in motion. The evidence for these beliefs is purely circumstantial, but nevertheless highly suggestive. Next, to say that children are innately equipped to learn *language* is, as we have seen, to say that they are equipped to learn a communication system with certain very restrictive defining characteristics. They will not, and perhaps cannot, learn a system based on a different 'algebra' from that of natural language. But the language of their parents displays not only qualities present in all languages, but also features peculiar to English, or Russian, or Swahili, or whatever. These features obviously have to be learnt by the child from the example of linguistically competent speakers around him; even so, he has some innate help in this problem, since his parents cannot use features which are precluded by the general laws of language design – laws which, if the biological thesis is correct, the infant 'knows' just as well as his elders.

The evidence from the practical study of languages suggests that languages may resemble one another fundamentally at the level of deep structure, and differ considerably, within generous but rigid limits, at the level of surface structure. Perhaps the infant learns the base grammar by developing his own inbuilt resources, and the *L*-specific, transformational component by example, imitation, practice and reinforcement, in interaction with members of the speech-community into which he happens to be born. Modern studies of the acquisition of syntax by children suggest that they learn structures describable by simple rewriting rules first, and later – often over quite an extended period – transformational structure. This is, admittedly, tangential evidence, and it is very difficult to interpret even under the best experimental conditions.

Now we turn to the implications for grammar-writing of our assumed linguistic universals. Clearly, the grammar has to represent what it is that the child eventually comes to learn when he has matured into a fully competent speaker of *L*. So just as the child's achievement is under universal constraints, so is the linguist's grammar: it refers to the design features of all language just as much as to the idiosyncratic properties of the *L* immediately under description. A particular grammar depends on a theory of universally necessary and permissible structure at three levels. The semantic component must reflect those categories and relations of meaning which are permitted by the structure of the human cognitive apparatus; the phonological component must draw on only those phonetic features and processes which are humanly articulatable and which are characteristic of human language; and the syntactic component must offer rules of kinds allowed by the universal design features of syntactic structure.

Chomsky has distinguished between *substantive* and *formal* linguistic universals. Although the exact dividing line between these two types is difficult to establish, the broad distinction is quite revealing. A substantive universal is a particular feature which *must* appear in every language. For instance, the phonemes of all languages are defined by reference to a fixed, finite set of phonetic variables which have precise articulatory specifications independent of any particular language. The phonetic 'substance' of every language must include sounds with a universal phonetic definition. Again, it has been suggested that every human language has a noun/verb (or, possibly, Subject/Predicate) distinction; if this is true, then it is a substantive universal. Formal universals are more abstract characteristics of language design. If all languages employ transformations, this is a formal universal. If transformational rules must always be ordered in their application, this is a formal universal. Another formal universal is that no language has 'structure-independent' transformations. A structure-independent T-rule would be such as the following:

$$A + B + C + D + E + F \Rightarrow F + E + D + C + B + A$$

in which the string is changed by the simple operation of linear reversal. In practice, transformations refer to linguistic structure, i.e. to P-markers not to the linear order of elements in strings.

A substantive universal of transformational processing would be that every language has, say, an apposition rule. Although that one seems an unlikely candidate, some other particular processes (e.g. negation) would seem to be candidates for substantive universals. In general, the form rather than the substance of T-rules is likely to be universally determined.

Ultimately, a particular grammar is best regarded as a kind of 'appendix' to universal grammar. If we ever discover what exactly is the content of universal grammar, then there will be many facts which we need not state afresh every time a grammar of a particular language is written. Quite possibly, the design of the base PSG, its categories and functions (see Chs. 3 and 4), will not need to be described separately for every language. The transformations will need to be described at length, since it is these which differentiate individual languages. But the conventions for the form and ordering of transformations will be universal facts, and this knowledge will allow substantial economies and increases in clarity and power to be achieved. Of course, we are a very long way indeed from understanding the universal principles of grammar: the study has only just begun. As we learn more about linguistic universals, the job of particular linguistic description will become much easier. Present problems, such as the one with which the previous chapter ended, will not need to be solved in terms of just the immediate material to be analysed – which is to say, in an utterly unprincipled way! Because of our present lack of knowledge of the forms of transformational rules, I have had to state hypothetical solutions to the descriptive needs of the data almost as if they were a mechanical response to the individual bits of data themselves. As more knowledge of the permitted *kinds* of rules is accumulated – or even knowledge of what rules operate in relevant areas of other languages – some types of solution will be seen as *a priori* acceptable or *a priori* improbable. At the moment, lacking a universal syntax, our analyses are bound to be tentative.

I hope it is obvious that this book does not claim to be an introduction to a single, agreed, version of transformational grammar: no such consensus exists, and, judging by the present state of linguistics (January 1971), perfection of TG is still a long way in the future. This book is based on a variety of ideas about TG drawn eclectically from a number of phases in the development of the subject and, deliberately, offers what might be considered a rather conservative model. In the last two or three years, several scholars – notably Emmon Bach, Charles J. Fillmore and James D. McCawley – have argued that the Chomskyan model of grammar must be radically revised. Their arguments are highly suggestive, but as yet do not fall into one consolidated position. Some clear general tendencies are emerging, however, and I will try to indicate these briefly; for a (probably premature) attempt at a synthesis, see Langendoen's *Essentials of English Grammar*.

In the 'classic' Chomskyan grammar, a *syntactic* base is proposed, and it is suggested that this base represents the 'deepest' universal features of language design. These fundamental properties include certain functional notions such as 'Subject' and 'Predicate', and certain category notions such as 'Noun', 'Verb' and 'Adjective'. As we have seen, the earliest stages of the derivation of a sentence entail the construction of one or more underlying phrase-markers, which are abstract syntactic objects whose structure can be expressed as a hierarchy of constituents; and the constituents are identified according to the categories they belong to and the functions they perform. Information about lexical content and semantic structure is given only after the phrase-structure rules have been applied (and before the transformations, according to Katz and Postal; but in our account the sequence is not so simple). In the grammar of *Aspects of the Theory of Syntax*, the base syntactic component is 'generative' and the semantic component 'interpretive' – the semantic component interprets syntactic objects, underlying phrase-markers: injects them with meaning. The new proposals for modifications to TG challenge that particular aspect of the model: it is now suggested that it is the *semantic* component which is generative. So at the 'deepest' level of representation, a sentence is a structure of meanings, not a syntactic structure.

The new model of generative grammar is perhaps most accessible in the work of Fillmore: see his papers 'The case for case' in Bach and Harms, *Universals in Linguistic Theory*, and 'Lexical entries for verbs' in the journal *Foundations of Language*, Vol. 4 (1968), pp. 373–93. Fillmore treats the *Predicate* as the basis of a sentence; for instance, the italicized word in

(405) He *hit* me on the head with a hammer.

is the Predicate of the sentence. Note that this is not the sense of 'predicate' invoked in the present book; it approximates closely to the use of 'predicate' in symbolic logic. The Predicate is, as it were, the semantic nucleus of a sentence. Apart from having a particular meaning (*hit* rather than *slap*, *strike*, etc.), the Predicate imposes a particular set of 'arguments' on a sentence. We can see from (405) that *hit* (similarly, *slap* and *strike*) may be accompanied by at least four arguments; and (405), taking this fact into account, may be represented symbolically as

$$P\ (a,\ b,\ c,\ d)$$

where $P \equiv hit$, $a \equiv he$, $b \equiv me$, $c \equiv on\ the\ head$ and $d \equiv with\ a\ hammer$. Fillmore suggests that each of the variables a, b, c, d performs a particular 'role' in relation to the Predicate: a is Agent, b Patient, c Location and d Instrument; and that these roles, or 'cases', may be drawn from a universal inventory of semantic categories. Notice that at least one other role, Time, can be added:

(406) He hit me on the head with a hammer *last Tuesday*.

and various roles can be deleted:

(407) He hit me on the head.
(408) He hit me with a hammer.
(409) He hit me.
(410) He hit me on the head last Tuesday.

Notice also that the roles remain the same despite permutation of surface structure:

(411) I was hit on the head last Tuesday.

Me is Patient in (410), *I* Patient in (411), though *me* is Object in (410), *I* Subject in (411). The survival of roles despite transformational processing explains some kinds of example which conventional TG finds particularly difficult to analyse; for instance, the cognitive synonymy of the following pair:

(412) John sold a car to Harry.
(413) Harry bought a car from John.

Let us assume that the role-structure is the same in each sentence – inventing roles, we could symbolize both as

$$P\ (\text{Source, Patient, Recipient})$$

In such an analysis, the differences of word-order, of prepositions, and of lexical items (*sell* vs. *buy*), are no longer embarrassing. *Sell* and *buy* could be said to have the same meaning, the same role-structure, but to require different transformational ordering of the variables.

It is obvious that, in this model of analysis, the functional notions 'Subject' and 'Object' relate to trivial aspects of surface structure. The difference in the treatment of Actives and Passives between Fillmore's case grammar and conventional TG is illuminating. Our analysis of (410) shows that the underlying and superficial Subjects are the same (*he*); but in (411) the superficial Subject (*I*) is not the underlying Subject. Fillmore dispenses with the notion 'underlying Subject': both (410) and (411) have Subjects, to be sure – *he* and *I* respectively – but 'Subject' is an entirely superficial notion; the underlying contrast is between Agent and Patient. The Subject is not restricted as to role: in (407)–(410) the Subject is the Agent, in (411) it is the Patient; in (414) it is the Instrument:

(414) A hammer hit me.

The same principle applies to Objects; contrast

(415) I'm eating a cake.
(416) I'm baking a cake.

In (415) the cake is in existence and something is done to it – it is Patient. In (416) the cake is caused to come into existence – it is Result. Arguably, it is more informative to distinguish (415) and (416) in these terms than to give them the same analysis – *the cake* the deep structure Object in both sentences – as conventional TG must do.

I have sketched out only one aspect of the new generative theory. Another effect which deserves scrutiny is the diminished reliance on lexical categories, as compared with standard TG. Just as the syntactic functions 'Subject' and 'Object' are subordinated to the roles 'Agent', 'Patient', etc., so also the lexical categories 'Noun', 'Verb', 'Adjective' are purely superficial notions – like 'Adverb' in our treatment. For example, Predicates may be typically Verbs (*hit*, *buy*, etc.), but they are not necessarily Verbs; compare these sentences:

(417) He teaches.
(418) He's a teacher.

Presumably we would want to say that these two sentences have the same underlying semantic structure. They make exactly the same statement about 'he': the difference is merely one of emphasis. The Predicate of (417) is clearly *teach* (and it is a Verb); and the most natural analysis of (418) makes *teacher* (a Noun) the Predicate. Let us say that the underlying representation of both sentences is:

TEACH, (he)

Although TEACH here looks like a verb, this is merely a morphological accident. If we allow the transformational component of the grammar the responsibility of distinguishing (417) and (418), then TEACH (as a Predicate) is quite neutral as to part of speech – the distinction between Noun and Verb is a feature of surface structure. In the present book, Noun and Verb are deep structure syntactic categories, but we have allowed that *N* and *V* may equally be exponents of our 'Predicate' (see p. 30 above) and that the 'verb *to be*' carries no semantic information (p. 30): the linguistic facts which our syntactic argument needed are equally relevant to the analysis of (417) and (418) in the generative semantic model. Similar arguments relating to the superficiality of the distinction between Verbs and Adjectives have to be considered in both generative syntax and generative semantics (see the discussion of 'stative' and 'non-stative' words in Lyons and elsewhere).

Thus, important areas of argument converge in generative syntax and generative semantics, and it could well be that the two models are not mutually destructive. Recently, Chomsky has claimed that generative semantics is no more than a 'notational variant' of the 'classic' transformational grammar with a generative syntactic base. This judgment seems a little harsh: there are certainly many insights in the new generative grammar which are not available in the conventional model (see (412)–(413), (415)–(416)). Current writings on the fundamentals of linguistic theory make it clear that the base of the traditional transformational grammar must sooner or later be revised so that it may attempt to capture 'deeper' universal cognitive categories than are at present accessible. However, these recent publications in generative semantics, or in case grammar, are obviously tentative and surely transitional. It is too early to cast overboard the sophisticated syntactic apparatus which has been developed in the last fifteen years – and no one has actually proposed this, despite the air of entrenched dichotomization in contemporary linguistics. Even in the generative semantic model, the present transformational syntax looks indispensable and secure.

But even if syntactic transformations retain their traditional importance in the new grammar, the argument about linguistic universals must be substantially different. I pointed out above (p. 168) that we lack a firm conception of universal syntax, so that many of our analyses have to be tentative at the moment. The 'generative semanticists' would argue that the syntactic universals proposed by Chomsky (and assumed by researchers in the field of infant language such as McNeill) are relatively weak compared with the semantic universals which may eventually emerge from the new model. Here the status of the 'roles' or 'cases' to which Fillmore has directed our attention is crucial. Although for the sake of argument roles at present have to be put forward in an arbitrary and *ad hoc* way (see my treatment of (412), (413)), it is obvious that they reflect very general categories of knowledge and, in a proper analysis, must ultimately be non-arbitrary. The roles reflect familiar attributes of the world human beings live in – a world of objects subject to certain spatio-temporal laws, of animate beings with properties and privileges; of actions, events, states, causes, effects. We could say that an analysis which presents language in terms of these categories recognizes the profound engagement of language with the way the world is organized, and hence the 'naturalness' of language. Fillmore makes it clear that he is prepared to connect his 'roles' with a theory of linguistic universals, a theory about the way human languages are 'constrained':

> I believe that human languages are constrained in such a way that the relations between arguments and predicates fall into a small number of types. In particular, I believe that these role types can be identified with certain quite elementary judgments about the things that go on around us: judgments about who does something, who experiences something, where something happens, what it is that changes, what it is that moves, where it starts out, and where it ends up. Since judgments like these are very much like the kinds of things grammarians have associated for centuries with the use of grammatical 'cases', I have been referring to these roles as case relationships, or simply, cases.
>
> ('Lexical entries for verbs', p. 382)

It seems clear that human languages must be structured in such a way that they allow us to talk about our world, using linguistic categories which fit the judgments about its mode of organization which we ordinarily make. (Note that we can take up this position without getting involved in fundamental epistemological, psychological or biological arguments about the *necessities* of human cognition – the case for 'case' does not prejudge the 'linguistic relativity hypothesis', for instance.) Case grammar makes available this class of linguistic universals in a natural and interesting way; we look forward to further systematization of the grammar of 'roles'.

Selected Reading

Because TG has developed rapidly and undergone substantial modifications, the chronology of publication of the books listed below is of the greatest importance. Students should take account of this principle when deciding in what order to arrange their supplementary reading.

1. *Major discussions*

N. Chomsky, *Syntactic Structures* (The Hague, 1957)

R. B. Lees, *The Grammar of English Nominalizations* (Bloomington, Indiana, 1960)

J. J. Katz and P. M. Postal, *An Integrated Theory of Linguistic Descriptions* (Cambridge, Mass., 1964)

N. Chomsky, *Aspects of the Theory of Syntax* (Cambridge, Mass., 1965)

U. Weinreich, 'Explorations in semantic theory', in T. A. Sebeok (ed.), *Current Trends in Linguistics*, III (The Hague, 1966)

P. S. Rosenbaum, *The Grammar of English Predicate Complement Constructions* (Cambridge, Mass., 1967)

E. Bach and R. T. Harms (eds.), *Universals in Linguistic Theory* (New York, 1968)

P. A. M. Seuren, *Operators and Nucleus* (London, 1969)

2. *Other works by Chomsky*

'A transformational approach to syntax', in A. A. Hill (ed.), *Proceedings of the Third Texas Conference on Problems of Linguistic Analysis in English, 1958* (Austin, Texas, 1962), pp. 124–58; reprinted in Fodor and Katz (see below), pp. 211–45

Current Issues in Linguistic Theory (The Hague, 1964). Also in Fodor and Katz, op. cit., pp. 50–118

Cartesian Linguistics (New York, 1966)

Selected Reading

Topics in the Theory of Generative Grammar (The Hague, 1966). Also in Sebeok, op. cit. (above), pp. 1–60

'The formal nature of language', Appendix A, pp. 397–442, in E. H. Lenneberg, *Biological Foundations of Language* (New York, 1967)

Language and Mind (New York, 1968)

(With Morris Halle) *The Sound Pattern of English* (New York, 1968)

3. Collections of articles

J. A. Fodor and J. J. Katz (eds.), *The Structure of Language* (Englewood Cliffs, N.J., 1964)

D. A. Reibel and S. A. Schane (eds.), *Modern Studies in English* (Englewood Cliffs, N.J., 1969)

R. A. Jacobs and R. S. Rosenbaum (eds.), *Readings in English Transformational Grammar* (Waltham, Mass., 1970)

M. Lester (ed.), *Readings in Applied Transformational Grammar* (New York, 1970)

J. Lyons (ed.), *New Horizons in Linguistics* (Harmondsworth, 1970)

4. Textbooks

E. Bach, *An Introduction to Transformational Grammars* (New York, 1964)

P. Roberts, *English Syntax* (New York, 1964)

O. Thomas, *Transformational Grammar and the Teacher of English* (New York, 1965)

A. Koutsoudas, *Writing Transformational Grammars* (New York, 1967)

R. A. Jacobs and P. S. Rosenbaum, *English Transformational Grammar* (Waltham, Mass., 1968)

D. T. Langendoen, *The Study of Syntax* (New York, 1969)

D. T. Langendoen, *Essentials of English Grammar* (New York, 1970)

5. General background

R. H. Robins, *General Linguistics: an Introductory Survey* (London, 1964)

R. H. Robins, *A Short History of Linguistics* (London, 1968)

J. Lyons, *Introduction to Theoretical Linguistics* (London, 1968)

175

Index

This is intended as an analytic guide to the contents, not as an exhaustive index (see Preface, p. viii). Major mentions, exemplifications and definitions of the main contents may be found here, but minor references are ignored. Definitions and examples should not be sought here.

177